I DON'T WANT YOU TO READ THIS

I DON'T WANT YOU TO READ THIS

a collection of essays my therapist was tired of listening to

Kiera Brynne

Contents

acknowledgments

To me –
who found the shaky courage
on a warm Texas day
to call myself a writer.

To my girls –
who see me when I cannot,
who breathe compassion and
grace into faltering lungs,
and who kiss and nurture my
bruised and broken heart.

To the artist –
who encouraged me to write naked,
who showed me the healing power of anger,
and who taught me that I will not *become* a writer;
I already am.

a note:

In college, I wrote my senior thesis about Jane Eyre, the protagonist and narrator of the classic novel by Charlotte Brontë.

I challenged that to misconstrue the audience, Jane proved to be an unreliable narrator. She sought to cast a flattering light only upon herself, damning others' reputations without divulging any faults of her own.

I may also prove to be an unreliable narrator, dear reader[1], as I write these autobiographical experiences. Memoirs can prove challenging to write—they are, to simplify their nature, snapshots of particular moments in time. They contain many experiences and result from reflections of years prior when their authors were under different types of emotional duress.

These are my snapshots.

My snapshots are neither impervious to mistakes nor perfect in their recollections. I am openly flawed and exceptionally hyper-aware of my shortcomings, which is why I have a therapist and a medium dose of anxiety meds.

As I seek to record my experiences in as much detail as I can remember, I acknowledge that I have shared only my side of these stories. I take the accounts of

---

[1]   Jane Eyre often uses the phrase "dear reader" to speak directly with her audience, so this is what's known as a joke.

the unnamed individuals in this book very seriously—
their perspectives may be strikingly different from
mine. I respect the sides of their experiences the
same way I respect my own, while still doing my
best to preserve the integrity of my memories.

you can find this book in the non-self-help section

an introduction

I wrote a book
rough-hewn and fragmented,
choppy and untimely paced,
like a life that is lived
with adventure and loss,
beauty and failure,
grace and defeat.

**I have nothing to say
and everything to say.**

> I follow no rules and
> present a story arc without an arc,
> with no real beginning
> and perhaps too many endings.

If all we ever really become are stories,
I don't want to be a "once upon a time"
or a "happily ever after."
I want to be wrapped up in the murk and greige
of the middle,
where real stories crystallize
under time and pressure.

Come to the middle with me.

a nametag

"Tell me about yourself."

Ew. Introductions are perplexing. The pressure to articulate a clever, witty representation of self is demanding: Provide just enough information to share a considerable chunk of one's identity without it sounding like a bad dating profile.

Not enough information? *Lacks a personality.* Too chatty? *Yikes. Pretentious and probably a serial killer.*

Most recently, in response to the armpit-sweat-inducing question, "What's your story?" I failed to present any charm or acumen and instead delivered an underwhelming ode to spicy queso. *Definitely a serial killer.*

Let's try this again:

"Hello, I'm Kiera."

I'm 37. I'm a woman, a writer, a sixth-grade teacher, a single mom of three girls, and a begrudging cat owner.

Boring.

"Hi, everyone. I'm Kiera."

I like tacos, laughing, and Olympic weightlifting, *and* I know most of the state capitals.

Wave. "I'm Kiera."

I'm a mediocre pickleball player, a size 10 shoe, a whirl of to-dos, a burgeoning introvert, and a practical joker. I have prematurely gray hair, am building an impressive sneaker collection, and enjoy a snarky quip and a quality oatmeal cream pie.

Is that enough?

"Hey! I'm Kiera."

I read when I feel like it. I can't wink, and I can barely whistle. I talk too loudly and eat too slowly. My favorite flowers are wildflowers native to the Wasatch Mountain Range. I will always put bacon and avocado on my sandwiches if that's an option. I watch movies and shows and ballets and symphonies and plays. I've got a million ideas but only about 50% follow through.

I believe in goodness. I hope for goodness. I pray for goodness.

"Yo. Kiera here."

I dislike confrontation. I fear innate laziness. It's important for me to know people's names. Bell peppers and mushrooms are disgusting. I make my bed every day. I shop on Amazon more than I should, and my credit score is reasonable.

"Aloha. This is Kiera."

I avoid small talk; instead, I feel power in real human connection. I trust people implicitly, believe in having hard conversations, and want lasting emotional intimacy. I crave the fear of new things, want to achieve the potential that stirs in me like magma, and desire always to see the good in humankind. I believe mistakes are a part of our stories, and I want the ability to always try again.

"Hola. Soy Kiera."

I want a home and an adventure, a life of simplicity, memories over things, a million more firsts, sunny days in the mountains, and mandatory sleep-in Sundays.

You see, I live in the margins. I'm a million words scattered across journal pages and post-it notes. The script I've written for my future is scrawled and annotated by a Ticonderoga #2 and rubbed raw with eraser shavings. I am not weighed down by the permanence of a Sharpie dictating whom I'm meant to be. I'm constantly (and I do mean constantly) rewriting the end of my story.

And I'd love to know:
What's your story?

i have no advice for you

I am a writer.

The decidedly non-expert kind.

The one without any advice.

Just a back-row, windows-down, hat-backward
girl who writes about understandings and
misunderstandings. Thoughts. About truths, the
real ones and the ones I thought were true until I
changed my mind. The kind of writer who writes
about transitions, about heavy, raw emotions
that are treacherous to navigate, and narrates
stories hidden by shame, betrayal, and grief.

I am sentences and poems, stories
and anecdotes, thoughts and wonders
bubbling through pages of real life.

I am a writer.

I write to remember.
I write so I can remember to share what I've learned,
about the messes and mess-ups,
the breaks and the stains and the
deep-seated bruises,
and about all the times when
I've said the wrong things
and done the wrong things
and been the wrong thing.

I write about the times I've been broken—
the times when I've healed,
and the times when I've stayed broken.

I am a writer.

The kind of writer who is afraid.

Always, always afraid that her words will burn you
or even worse,
that her words may never burn at all.

I am a writer.

Lit up by delicious words as bright and suggestive as
metropolitan marquees. I capture memories in tender
capsules swirling with vibrant colors. I gather strength
and courage at glowing words that crackle and spit
as if from a campfire. I find meaning and beauty in
the nuances of the words as dim as a firefly's glow.

I am a writer.

I doodle on napkins and the palms of my hands. I
hurriedly scratch ideas on post-it notes and litter
grocery lists with epiphanic thought downloads.

Piles of perforated notebook paper
ripped from their spirals
and graffitied with bright Paper Mate pens
whisper anecdotes,
shout sense and nonsense,
beg me to finish them,
to tell their stories
of lessons and laughs,
of lyrics and whispers.

I am a writer.

I see humanness and realness and stillness
and it surprises me and
wires me and
desires me,
and I write and scribble and jostle miscellany;
a piñata of words, colors, and ideas
ready to explode.

I am a writer.

I write how I've learned.

in pieces.
in bursts.
in shades of color.
in imperfection.
in shadows.
in power.
in grief.

I am a writer,

and I don't want you to read this.

oh, and also

I am scared.

Scared not only to write these whispers
and whirlwinds of the past,
but to have you read the words that bend
and amend, flatter and flower.

Words, you see, are tricky, and they
tempt and twist and tamper
as we feel the drum of our heartbeats
and we resin the bows to play
orchestras of our heartstrings.

But what if we need to see?

Because words beckon and build
and break us to pieces.
They sway as porch swings in gentle breezes
and sing us to sleep when we tuck ourselves into bed.

Words anger and agitate and amplify
and, really, they mean nothing at all
while at the same time meaning
damn near everything.

They hurt. And they heal. And they hurt. And they heal.

And just because it's written doesn't mean it's
who I am or
what I am or

why I am or
where I am.

There are no perfect words.

And so, I write imperfect words
for an imperfect life
that I am learning so imperfectly.

part 1:
the girl from the trailer park

"You need not be sorry for her.
She was one of the kind that likes to grow up.
In the end she grew up of her own free will
a day quicker than the other girls."

— J.M. Barrie, *Peter Pan*

judith anne drive

I lived in the nicest trailer park in town.

I mean, CLEARLY, it was a winner, with its convincing mantra of "Live the Good Life" and a current Google Review of 3.9 stars. Real high-brow mediocrity, am I right?

A real swell guy named Don managed the park. Don? Dan? I'll have to check with my dad. Anyway, [insert name here] ran the nicest trailer park in the biz. We were located on the corner of classy and trashy, and the uppity trailer parks were a wee bit difficult to come by.

The entrance to the park was bright and clean, the lawn neatly manicured. Fresh paint coated street signs and low fences containing mulch-piled pansies. Even the whole street-view row of single-wides looked as pristine as the rest of the entrance.

Upon traveling deeper inside the neighborhood and past the smiling and waving front staff, the façade of the park faded, like the paint on the shed that was allocated as a bus stop. Upon closer inspection, the white paint was chipped and hastily brushed, while swear words inked the shed walls and were carved into the wood posts—the good swear words too. The words that then became the topic of conversation at home when I asked, "What does [bleep] mean?" And then there would be a whole hubbub about the downfall of good Christian society, et cetera.

My brain rattled in my head as I biked over classic Indiana potholes that seemed to deepen out of spite and made trailer park mommas shout safety warnings out of front doors. I remember a particular moment when a curly-haired girl named Amber double-flipped me off (you know, using both hands) and confidently roller-skated away, only to then pitch over a particularly deep pothole.

I spent my childhood climbing trees in our yard and catching buckeyes falling from neighbors' trees. The buckeye-catching always included the hypervigilant "You-know-buckeyes-are-really-poisonous-and-if-you-eat-them-then-you'll-DIE-a-painful-death-here-try-one" conversation, which made my mom super mad. When we weren't trying to kill each other off by enticing the other with toxic buckeye stew, my brothers and I chased geese and caught bluegills in the murky pond behind the trailer park, which also held a small patch of grass with a pathetic-looking swing-set and a metal death slide. The heat from the summer sun made sliding down the slide akin to sliding down a cheese grater, so basically, it was really enjoyable.

Running parallel to the pond lay railroad tracks, heavy trains rattling through the corn-covered landscape most afternoons. My brothers and I spent plenty of time placing rocks and pennies on the tracks in our evil plot to take down the coal cars, booing each time the trains ceased to derail (which was every time).

We had full run of that trailer park. We biked and scoured the oddly named streets (e.g., Thelma, Bill, Bob, Gary, Judith Anne) for adventure and friendship. On the whole, we found hordes of kids. We ran through crotchety neighbors' yards and made friends with whoever's parents had a sprinkler running. The kids we were drawn to were usually much older than us, which meant they taught us all sorts of interesting words and foreign behaviors that absolutely delighted my mother.

I spent eight trailer park years skinning my knees on loose gravel and wading through the flooded streets during heavy thunderstorms when the drains would clog with street debris. I climbed trees with my brothers in bare feet and probably almost died many, many times.

Part of me is still a trailer park girl.

I can't ever, ever lose her.

keeping up

My brothers often ran off with a crude neighborhood boy— an oversized, paunchy kid named Matt. Matt was a fascinating character with an inordinate amount of knowledge about where and when to use his middle finger. He amended Frankie Laine's "Rawhide" with lyrics such as, "keep those big butts rollin'," which blew my third-grade, rule-following, formative mind because I was absolutely not allowed to use the word "butt."[2]

One particularly warm summer morning, Matt and my brother Aaron took off through the neighbors' lawns. Our single-wide trailer felt perpetually crowded with my parents' seven children running, shoving, and toddling across the peeling laminate floor. Aaron fled the chaos often, and I, in my entitled state, thought that surely, he'd also want ME to come along— his dirty, fledgling whip of a sister. All dark, ratty hair to match my scabbed knees and mettlesome personality.

I was, in my memory, raised as a boy until I was six years old, when my longed-for sister came along. I remember trying to pee outside in the woods and

---

[2]   I still remember the day I learned that "butt" is not an actual swear word like my parents purported it to be. Many words were off-limits: "God," "Geez," "Shut up," "Crap." Especially "fart." Mom made us use the word "pootle" when we had to, you know, pootle. To this day, I am scarred by its usage.

run around shirtless at the park, finding it terribly unfair that I had to SIT DOWN when I used the toilet.

Barefoot and slender, I chased the boys down the hot asphalt until my calloused feet burned. I skipped through yards and gathered dandelions for bright, chummy bouquets until I found the boys stashed in the corner of the neighborhood, looking annoyed at the unkempt sister following at their heels.

"You can only hang with us if you can keep up," Matt said, eyeing me. Aaron nodded in agreement.

Challenge accepted, boys.

They ran through the trailer park, throwing rocks into the pond to scare the tiny bluegills that lived in the dredges of the dirty shore. They chased the geese that flocked in our way and skillfully gathered tadpoles in the mucky streams by the buckeye trees.

And I kept up.

Until I had to pee.

This presented a problem.

But I had to keep up with the boys. So, I held it, as idiot children do. My seven-year-old bladder was doing its best, but my obnoxious tenacity was pushing it until I was on the brink of melting into a large puddle.

I was two streets from home. It was not practical to run back home in this event. Not only would my body most likely rupture on the way, but also, the chances were high that my mom would probably make me stay and help her with the laundry.

I've always been a pretty good problem solver, you know. Resourceful, even. So, I did what any stubborn, self-respecting, socially awkward girl in the early 90s would do:

I peed my pants in a stranger's yard.

She wasn't a "stranger," per se. She was the genial old lady two streets over who always gave out Milk Duds for Halloween and whose garden boxes were full of faded silk flowers. I grabbed the hose coiled carefully on the house mount; the spigot squealed as I turned it on. I hosed down my soaked shorts, grabbed a drink (hoses are so multipurpose when one is young), and scrammed to find those boys. I'm pretty sure I even left the hose on like a damn ungrateful fool. To this day, I wonder: Why did that woman have a hose if all her flowers were fake?

I caught up to Matt and Aaron, my lungs burning from the Indiana humidity and the exhaustion of "keeping up."

"What happened to you?" they asked, looking at the water dripping water down my legs from my saturated shorts.

"Got hot," I lied.

They shrugged, and I ran to grab buckeyes from the base of the shady trees, proud of truly earning my pass to the Trailer Park Bro Sesh.

dummy brothers

Due to the forever lack of funds that help buy things
(like a washer, for example), my mom would haul
loads and loads of dirty clothes to my Grandma
Connie's house every Monday to do the laundry.
Luckily for my mom, Grandma lived only three
streets behind us and saved us from the boredom
of spending our entire days at a laundromat.

Monday laundry days were long days. We had
seven kids under ten years old, and my mom
used cloth diapers. Yeah. It was TERRIBLE.

Even when we would travel the extended
walk to Grandma's after the bus dropped
us off at the graffitied bus stop, Mom
still wasn't done with the laundry.

It took FOREVER.

One sunny Monday, as we were waiting impatiently
for Mom to finish, my brothers disappeared. I
didn't care; I didn't like them anyway. I was sitting
at Grandma's glass and wicker dining room
table, and my mom's voice broke the silence.

"Kiera, will you go check on your brothers? I
haven't seen them in a while. Go make sure
they're not getting in trouble," my mom said.

Pause. Um. I was playing Uno with myself, and
I was winning. Also, I didn't care if they WERE

getting in trouble. She was asking for a serious sacrifice here because I was about to Draw 4 myself—I had some serious strategy on hand.

"Kiera. Go do what I ask," she repeated, exasperated. That's pretty much the adjective I'd describe my mom for the entirety of my childhood. Exasperated at my delicate qualities of defiance and snark. Maybe add a little shake of turbulent emotional intelligence under the "great qualities" section of my childhood resume.

I grumbled as I walked outside. I grumbled as I kicked open Grandma's door. I stewed in frustration as I walked outside and yelled for those stupid boys. I felt so irritated.

Until.

I saw the dummies doing the dummy thing. The dummiest thing you can imagine.

I smiled maniacally, my thin lips twisting into a Grinch-esque grin. I was elated. Sinisterly elated.

A little background: My grandma and uncle recycled their glass beer bottles and had bags and bags of them leaning against the backyard shed. (In curiosity's hindsight, I actually wonder why they had so many bags? Did my sarcastic, introverted, soap-opera-watching Grandma throw massive ragers with all her pinochle-playing friends? That classy broad. RIP, girl.)

And my dummiest dummy brothers had decided in the channel of wisdom that ran through their tiny brains that they would use these beer bottles in a productive, environmental kind of way. By LOBBING THEM at the girl neighbor who stood behind the fence that demarcated the trailer park's property line. (Did you forget that we were in a trailer park? NEVER FORGET.)

Boys. Beer bottles. Big problem.

Brilliant.

Oh, how mightily I stood, leaning against the outside trailer wall. I was like a queen in my yellow and white striped romper as I taunted my brothers with the classic, "I'm going to tell Mom, and you are going to be in so much trouble." I felt vindicated and superior in my role of Tattle-Tale. Who needed Uno? —I had won the sibling game. Checkmate, bruhs. I was going to be the hero, the favored of the exasperated mother.

I relished it. I breathed it in, their upcoming spankings. And it was ALL in my control. I could go inside at any moment and let the woman know what HER sons had done.

Oh. I was in love with this thing called power.

But then.

The next few sounds seemed to have all happened at once. A car door slammed. Another bottle smashed. A girl cried.

My brothers had thrown another bottle at the fence. The girl beyond had cut her hand on a broken piece of glass. Guttural rage was heard.

Oh, shit.

Dad is here.

Let us pause for a moment of reflection. Before you make a hasty judgment call on my dad, you need to know this. He is a giant of a man. At 6'6" and 400 pounds for most of my life, coupled with his incredibly loud voice, his stature is immediately intimidating. However, my dad is, hands-down, one of the nicest people I know. He's incredibly loving and a good listener, and he always challenged us to be more than we were, which, at the moment, was a group of vandals.

However, when he appeared after work to help finish the laundry and saw that his dummy sons and his quite lovely daughter were at the scene of a beer-bottle-throwing crime, Dad's rage suddenly matched his stature.

First thought: Survival. GET OUT OF THE WAY. Run for the border. Hide behind Grandma's cacti plants. Pretend to be an orphan.

To no avail.

Before you could say "Dad's-face-is-purple-watch-out," we were lined up in front of Dad getting ready for some good old-fashioned spankings.

"I didn't do anything!" I protested loudly. "Aaron and Mark were throwing the bottles, and I was just going out to check on them because Mom told me to!" I was fuming. Steam escaped my juvenile ears. I was getting a Dad-handed spanking (read: giant hands) because my dumb brothers did something totally pea-brained.

But then Mom served me a giant blow: "Why didn't you come in right away and tell me when it was happening?"

What. A. Traitor.

Um, what happened to Girl Power, Mom? Ovaries before brovaries? I had been utterly betrayed. The woman clearly was, again, exasperated at my power-hungry method of holding my brothers' delicate future in the balance of my elementary hands.

Mom had Benedict Arnold'ed me. I had lost.

I squirmed. I fought. I yelled. But the big-mitt spanking ensued. To be honest and even more critical of this 27-year-old historical event, I ended up with a worse punishment than my brothers because I had known the extent of the situation and hadn't said a single thing. To this day, I don't know what's tattling and what's not. I'm bereft of joy in my old age because of this.

Those dummy brothers.

Epilogue: Later in the week, we (YES, INCLUDING ME) had to head three streets back to my grandma's house to pick up all the glass that NOT ME threw. It took hours and hours of scouring the grass to find all the pieces of the amber-colored bottles.

I filled my large sack with glass and picked it up to throw it into the bin at the end of the driveway.

Pause here.

Young kid, picking up an overstuffed
bag full of heavy glass.

The weight of the bag coupled with some sort of
scientific term about velocity and centrifugal force
or something (maybe I was swinging it?) caused
a jagged piece of glass to slam into my right calf,
creating a gash that bled like a war wound.

I still have a scar. Still bitter. Still bereft of joy.

Those dummy brothers.

picking out pennies

A particular moment stands out to me just now.

It's a short, unassuming story but is a compelling reminder of the often-impossible decisions demanded of us in parenthood and adulthood.

———————————

My childhood piggy bank was a ceramic pig, cast and hand-painted by my quirky, orange-haired grandmother. The pig itself was dull and unmemorable, except it stood on its hind legs and held flowers in its chunky, non-opposable pettitoes.

I didn't watch the hammer hit the piggy banks or hear the crash of broken pieces falling to the table.

I knew its demise was coming; my parents had gently explained that we were in some difficult financial straits and the insignificant amounts from our piggy banks would help cover some immediate costs.

I peeked through the door of the bedroom that I shared with five of my other siblings. My dad, as I've described him before, was a huge man in stature and heart and sat quietly in the dining room alcove of our single-wide trailer, sifting through the remnants of the shattered remains.

The silver coins had already been sorted and piled to the side.

I watched my dad pick out pennies
from the clay wreckage.

Pennies.

He needed pennies from the same children
for whom he was trying to provide.

The trauma of this experience has weighed on him for
over thirty years.

———————————

I think often of the necessary humility that moment
demanded of my parents, the guilt that may
have writhed internally, the pain of inadequacy
felt by my dad—like he wasn't enough.

I wonder if he knows how often I pick out the
proverbial pennies from my own wreckage, collecting
the small tokens, the minute, the seemingly worthless
moments that could slowly add up to being enough.

I wonder if he knows that his example of
sacrifice creates a tender glow over the
hardship-stricken memories of my youth.

I wonder if he knows I'm glad I had
the pennies to give him.

Take all my pennies, Dad.

inconvenience

Her little body floated face-down on top of the water.

She wasn't moving.

I remember thinking she looked like one of those long-legged water bugs that skim weightlessly across the surface of stagnant water.

The small pool was new, the summer sun warming the cold hose-water filling its capacity. Before long, dried grass and dead bugs would coat its clear surface, dragged in by asphalt-burned bare feet.

I remember this image clearly, this moment frozen in time—imprinted upon the film of my formative memories.[3]

I can't remember, though, who was supposed to be watching her.

I grabbed her slender arm and pulled her upright. She gasped for air, sputtering through the wet hair that had gathered into a glob on her face.

"Don't do that," I snapped.

---

[3] Apparently, though, I never told anyone about this, not even my mom. As I was writing this story, a whole hullabaloo broke loose and now my sister owes me for unknowingly saving her life.

The snapshot of that particular moment resurfaces in my subconscious often, along with a specific tendril of thought that heightens the reality and weight of that experience:

What would have happened if I hadn't been there?

monsters

When I was a little girl
and slept on the top bunk
in a crowded, wood-paneled bedroom,
I'd dream of monsters.

When the fireflies turned out their lights
and fluorescent street lamps glowed warily,
I'd squint into the nothingness
of the witching hour
and feel the quickening thumps of my heart.

Skewed refractions of light
cast menacing shadows of unfamiliar creatures
onto walls and pillowcases,
while the muffled snoring down the hall
was surely a dragon's roar.

And it would seem that the Sandman
has missed the little girl
tucked tightly into the corner of an old bunk,
a frayed blanket gathered
around the nape of her neck.

"Go away!" I'd plead quietly
to the monsters, complicit
in forcing their way through my defense
as they lurked along walls,
in dresser drawers,
under beds,
and behind doors.

When I was a little girl,
I felt anxiety for the very first time
as it manifested itself
as irrational fears
and uneasy abstraction.

And it was easy, too easy,
to learn to let them in,
to allow the monsters who walled me in the darkness
take up coveted, permanent space
inside my growing mind.

When I was a little girl,
I'd dream of monsters.

I still do.

a house made of zip ties and duct tape

I stood at the edge of my parent's driveway, wrestling with deep-seated demons as I stared at my childhood home. I exhaled.

Nothing has changed, I thought.

The driveway asphalt had cracked from indecisive Indiana climes, crumbling into slippery gravel. Mildew ran the length of the vinyl siding, and years of humid condensation had found a home in the hidden crevices. The roof had collected leaves and debris, where small saplings germinated from windblown helicopter seeds. Wood rot disintegrated window trim while cobwebs inhabited window frames; light fixtures were insect graveyards, long past dead. The metal horse weathervane, bent from an errant baseball, sat on top of the garage trusses, still standing after all these years.

When I was in fourth grade, in a desperate effort for home ownership, my parents had purchased a decades-old, builder-grade two-story with a failed home inspection. Water drainage issues and botched electrical work, the inspector said.

A challenge, my dad had decided. Extremely resourceful in a MacGyver-like kind of way, coupled with a degree in electrical engineering, he had a certain self-confidence in fixing things that couldn't be fixed. He taught me how to jury-rig just about anything.

Twenty years had passed since I had wandered the house's then-pristine halls, bright with new paint; then, the carpets had been clean and new—for the only time in two decades.

This home was its own kind of Giving Tree.

Twenty years of ten children wounding its structure and integrity, with its too many people in too small of a space. Twenty years of crowding around the old oak table for family dinners— a sort of overfill that was both physically uncomfortable and deeply nostalgic. This home had burst at its literal seams as it had tried to hold its many loud, demanding inhabitants.

At ten years old, whimsy and exploration saturated my formative years. The third of an acre of our own property was a lush upgrade from the old asphalt driveway of the trailer park. My brothers and I caught lightning bugs in the backyard, chasing each other through long grass and clover. Chiggers bit at our ankles, while the humidity gifted perpetual sweat on our necks. The apple trees grew bushy by the farm behind the house, and we dreamed of building treehouses in its thick branches. We picked wild blackberries for Mother's Day, pricking our thumbs on thorny vines. Stout, royal Chinese Elms shaded the brick patio, and we raked the whirlwinds of leaves that dropped every autumn into towering piles of bronze and marmalade.

I couldn't imagine living anywhere else.

Within years of moving in, our house began to tilt due to an unstable water table. The foundation cracked, causing fissures to splinter across floors and walls. Ten kids hopscotched over rapidly growing holes in the floor as the older boys were in charge of pumping extraneous water out of the claustrophobic crawl space.

As youth made way for adolescence, the house fell into greater disrepair. The pride I felt for our family home quickly dissipated, and shame took hold of the void.

Cold air seeped in through the windows, the latches and mechanisms rusty and broken. AC units butted out of the second story, quick fixes to solve a more expensive problem. The four-leaf clovers that had enchanted us as children now choked the grass and the elms swayed dangerously over the roof and powerlines. Soon, trees were hewn and relegated to the enormous burn pile. A weathered playhouse in the backyard housed more wasps than children, and a lonely burnt-out grill was the only occupant of the brick patio. Makeshift graves of old pets dotted the backyard: a loved but neglected dog, countless cats whose jobs had been to catch the mice that made nests in the walls, and a few cranky hamsters. Overgrown ivy climbed the side of the house, and rusty, flat-tired bicycles with ripped seats and missing chains leaned against the crumbling brick.

I rarely invited friends over.

Our home was broken.

Holes pock-marked the drywall by angry brothers and broken pipes, and water leaked through ceiling plaster, causing drenched, swollen pockets to pucker precariously over our heads. Kids picked sneakily at peeling wallpaper, tearing off curled, inconsistent strips. Inexpensive wood paneling still lines the walls of the family room to this day. Only one shower worked, and we got used to the rusty well water that stained our whites and prickled our tongues with its sulfur taste. Blankets hung in bedroom doorways as makeshift doors —the hollow wooden doors hadn't lasted long— while we opened any remaining doors with flathead screwdrivers. Wooden banisters, wobbly from missing balusters, waited impatiently for repair, and broken light fixtures collected thick layers of dust over years of disuse.

I was in 6th grade when we bought a piano. A beautifully lacquered, walnut-colored piano that sat as a distraction in the midst of chaotic dilapidation.

I sat at the piano, staring at its clean, glossy keys.

For a moment, its polished simplicity distracted me from the truth that surrounded me, the shame that suffocated me.

But when I turned around, nothing had ever changed.

Once, my 7th-grade bus driver told me he'd pay me $75 for my house.

I told him I'd take it.

I stood, staring at this house held together by zip ties and duct tape.

Humiliation and embarrassment tinged my dad's face as he grew too overworked and tired to keep up with its endless maintenance. Shame burdens its wooden bones, failure seeps into its very foundation. The house creaks under pressure, and even the roof strains under the weight of disgrace.

I feel uneasy as I whisper to you the secrets of this old house. We have carried the weight of thousands of its crumbling bricks for far too long.

Every word I write feels like a personal betrayal.

I couldn't possibly write all of them.

But, also.

This house was my home.

I learned to love so deeply inside its weathered walls.

I learned about forgiveness.

I hope this house forgives me, too.

a rubbery tale

This may surprise you (if you've read up to this point, it definitely won't), but popularity really eluded me as a youth, especially in those obscure middle school years.

If I'm being fair, I got along with lots of people, yes. I've always been able to talk to just about anyone. Mostly the senior citizen Walmart greeters who hand out smiley face stickers to passersby. I always got LOTS of stickers.

Yet, as is the case today, in every school are the kids with inward demons of their own who take out their frustrations on awkward, clique-less kids.

Like me.

I fit in as a misfit, a bit socially inept, eclectically dressed with rerun hand-me-downs, ashamed of my place on the lowest rung of the socioeconomic ladder. I had grown quickly, and my physical abilities were subpar. I tried out for the volleyball team and was given the position of secondhand team manager— a polite way of saying "thanks, but no thanks." I wasn't quite sure how to move my flailing, disjointed limbs in a way that didn't resemble a panicked Woody from Toy Story.

Wishy-washy with my own integrity, I made friends and sometimes lost them as I waffled between goodness and dishonesty. I felt alone much of the time, sometimes of my own choosing and sometimes because I wasn't sure how to break the barrier of pre-established, tight-knit friend groups.

I relied on relationships with my teachers because I knew they'd accept me, love me, and find the best in me. Sidebar: Maybe that's why I chose to teach.

Regardless, I was a bullseye for teasing.

One cold January morning in 8th grade, my class ventured out of the classroom for an outdoor winter project. Dressed in oversized khaki flares, an ill-fitting purple blouse, and strappy black dress shoes, I ignored everyone as they whispered and tittered about my frozen red toes in the freezing January air. I found a bench to sit on, my frozen feet burning from having lost any sort of circulation.

Behind me, I heard boys giggling in their prepubescent guffaws, obviously ignoring the teacher's instructions. I rolled my eyes. That sort of behavior always annoyed me. While I inevitably thought it was okay to disrespect my mom every day (you can ask her—I was a pro), I could never disrespect a teacher's authority in the classroom. To me, teaching was a type of social standing that demanded an extremely high regard.

I felt movement behind me as the stupid, chortling boys approached my forest green bench.

Moments later, I felt an egg-like fluid pour down my long, lanky hair. The scent of acetone and alcohol permeated the air around me. I reached up instinctively and touched the

sticky, viscous liquid that had already leached
into my scalp and drowned my roots.

Rubber cement. They had poured rubber
cement over the top of my head.

The boys ran off, laughing derisively.

I froze.

There's this moment, you know? This moment
that feels infinitely long where a person
has an impossible decision to make.

Some people fight.
Some people flee.

I always freeze.

I looked at my hands covered in rubbery glue. The
cold air stung my face as gobs of gelatinous cement
saturated my hair. The more curious, perhaps more
compassionate students had gathered around and
were picking out the rubbery remnants from my scalp.

I didn't have much to say.

I couldn't decide if I was grateful or mortified.

I'll fast-forward the rest of the story. The teacher
saw what happened (I hold that gratitude very
close to my chest), the boys got in trouble,
and I got an apology letter the next day.

Et cetera.

But that eternal moment where I had to choose my response—I'll always remember feeling the delayed shift inside my brain, heavy cogs reversing, the clunks and clinks of switching gears.

Twenty-five years later, I still freeze. I still sit and stare at the ground as I process the unexpected and wait for the cognitive mechanics to recalibrate.

Maybe one day, I'll deliver a hefty series of superhero sucker punches or run away until the pressure in my lungs dissipates.

But most likely you'll find me sitting right here.

Frozen in response, but, this time, glue-free.

flaps

He had a thick, hairy neck.

An odd detail to remember, since I
can't even remember his name.

Let's call him Carl. I don't know anything about Carl,
except that he liked to smoke in the ditch by the buses
after school, and he wore glasses with thick lenses
because his eyes were uncharacteristically squinty.

Carl sat next to me during middle school PE
class. Not because he wanted to. His last name
probably started with a letter unfortunately
close to H and, clearly, he suffered for it.

PE meant school-issued uniforms: mid-thigh green
gym shorts, drawstring waistband folded down at
least twice to give those boys a nice peep of the gams.
Add a shapeless gray t-shirt with HURLEY marked
on it in chiseled Sharpie—I was walking perfection.

This particular day wasn't extraordinary,
just another gym period I would've liked to
avoid. I dressed quickly and hurried to blend
into the sea of forest green shorts.

This time, though, Carl decided
to be a ruthless little jerk.

He stood in front of the line of his peers, and
with some sort of over-peaked confidence,

declared that he would be the God of deciding who had cool shoes, 1997 edition.

Oh, shit.

He started with the front of the line. I started sweating.

"Yeah, you've got cool shoes. Yep. You too." Carl pointed and succinctly grunted at the kids with shoes that, you know, didn't suck. Nikes and Adidas and K-Swiss (which, okay? They look like you're wearing small suitcases on your feet, Carl).

I tucked my feet underneath me as naturally as I could, trying to hide my Sasquatch-sized babies. I can't. I mean, literally.

Also, important to note: As Judgy McCarl made his rounds, I remember thinking, *Why are you acting like the king of cool shoes? You haven't made the rounds of popularity necessary for this kind of judgment.*

Then he walked up to me, sauntering a little. Carl looked for my shoes. I kept my head down, letting this punk infect me with shame. I couldn't even look at his stupid, squinty eyes.

As previously and redundantly established, my clothes and shoes often ran through a couple of kids–and probably through the hands of most Goodwill employees—before they got to me. Dated shirts and worn-through jeans; I was an icon of "What Not to Wear."

These shoes were no exception.

Aged, murky Reeboks. Hand-me-downs from my mom. A shade of used-to-be white, now hinting deliciously of the kind of gray that stains the teeth of lifelong smokers. These kicks were definitely retro, except 20 years too late and 20 years too early. Right in the middle of the "Kiera is not cool" movement.

They were spongy and dingy, all the markings faded. The tread had worn off completely, so I was an acrobatic sideshow in any sort of slick weather. The shoelaces were broken off, so they couldn't be tied super securely. When I stepped fully into the shoe, the heels and ball of my foot settled into the worn holes.

But the worst parts were the flaps.

The adhesive securing the bottom of the shoes had worn off, which meant that the tired soles weren't at all fastened to the actual shoes themselves. With each step I took, both shoes flapped.

Flapping, dingy, broken shoes. Literal "flap-flops."

And here came Carl with his self-appointed shoe superiority.

"Your shoes suck," he snickered, pointing at my hidden shoes.

My cheeks reddened, and shame took a front-row seat, where it stayed for decades to follow.

to all the people from whom I stole

It wasn't personal.

It was simple.

I saw what you had—it was what I didn't.

Babysitting gave me access, and
I gave myself permission.

Sports bras pulled from closets and eyeliner
nicked from bathroom drawers, Pop-Tarts and
Pringles stuffed in coat pockets, CDs and movies
from entertainment centers, quarters from hidden
troves above the fridge, gift cards from drawers.

I learned to lie to my mom to cover up for the influx
of new personal items, and I wore your clothes, your
jewelry, and the makeup I pilfered from your homes.

I can't tell you the day I stopped stealing, but
one day, I just stopped. Cold turkey. Flipped
the switch. Now I can't even walk out of a
grocery store with unpaid-for cream cheese.

All this to say:

I'm sorry.

Love,
A klepto

roses

I write this carefully.

I spent most of my middle and high school years on a stage.

At 17, music had become the most powerful component of who I was. From playing cello to acting and singing in musicals and choir concerts—I had found a rich community, a safe place that helped an awkward, misfit teenage girl find incredible confidence, mentors, and, for the first time, friends. I felt alive, determined, and challenged to nurture a beautiful talent that I still use to connect with others in the same way (and I still don't need a mic).

This deep commitment of mine wasn't easy on my mom. As a parent of ten kids, she was embattled with chauffeuring us to our several thousand extracurricular activities. I waited constantly in school vestibules as the nights darkened, looking for her headlights as she rushed to pick me up from rehearsals that ran late.

I took up so much of her time, but she was always there.

Always present at every concert.
Musical. Play. Banquet. Everything.

She sat close to the front to hear me sing, but post-concert, she relegated herself to the quiet spot by the pillar of the library as she waited patiently for me (although perhaps not as patiently as I remember).

On a post-performance high, my friends and I would run to the large high school foyer, where the attendees would spill out after the concerts. We'd laugh and share in the bright acclamations of success while humbly acknowledging genuine compliments echoing around us. Parents and grandparents would laden singers' arms with favorite treats and bouquets of reds, whites, yellows, and pinks.

Roses.

I saw it. I felt it.

The discomfort that churned in my stomach wasn't new; those subtle pangs of "we can't afford it" had sat ashamedly for many years.

One of ten kids. One of ten kids.

I had forever lived a life of staunch necessity. Anything extra was superfluous. It was enough, to be a part of this community that had embraced me and buoyed me up. And, simply, I just couldn't have what others had.

Meaning: I'd never get the roses.

"Are you ready, Sweetie?" my mom would ask as the cumulative goodbyes and well-dones and tired smiles dwindled. Everyone left, their brightly jeweled roses cradled tenderly in the crooks of their arms.

"I'm ready, Mom."

———————————

High school came to an end. Our last choir concert was emotional, especially for those of us who had found a makeshift home and impenetrable friendships in this little niche. I shared in the after-concert joys and communal celebrations, and looked over the heads of a million people as I tried to find my mom by the library pillar.

"Are you ready, Sweetie?" She hugged me tightly. I was surprised as she handed me a slender bundle wrapped in crinkled cellophane.

I looked at her in absolute wonder, and I immediately cradled the bouquet tenderly in the crook of my arm.

They weren't roses.

In my arms lay three light pink carnations, the stem of one bent and misshapen, the flowers most likely leftover from the nearby discount bin.

I froze as I clung to the carnations. My head spun. My chest welled with humble, grateful pride. I was going to burst. For my mom. For the absolute power of her sacrifice. For her wanting to give me more than she ever could.

"I remember feeling bad that they weren't roses," she told me once.

———————————

My two eldest daughters each picked out small bouquets of flowers for my youngest daughter's first ballet recital today.

We sifted through colorful bouquets filled with jewel-toned roses and baby's breath. Lilies. Snapdragons and daisies. Queen Anne's Lace.

We picked carnations.

I always pick carnations.

report card comments

Written on every report card:

Kiera is a pleasure to have in class.

What it might say one day:

Kiera is wild. A rebellious, loyal leader who stands up for others and breaks idiotic social norms while filling hearts with desire and calls to action. She pushes others to be better. She inspires others to find courage. She breaks barriers and smashes through what we expected of her. She fails continually, and through her failure, she finds different ways to succeed. She is never done. She exists in a sphere of perpetual connection as she strives to build a safe, inclusive place for those around her. She's different. She's fierce. Untamed. Trapping her in convention will rouse the fire that made her.

She's not a pleasure to have in class; she's the change we need.

part 2:
happily ever after and its antithesis

"She let the [compass] needle swing
north and watched it settle true.
She held it against her heart. Where
else would one need a
compass more than in this place?"

—Delia Owens, *Where the Crawdads Sing*

broken bridges, part 1

We sat upon the clouds, he and I.

A future, we said. Bright and elegant,
constructed from our fledgling dreams and
unassuming hopes and dashes of whimsy.

Hand in hand, we collected tiny concepts and
bursts of intuition and kept them safe in our pockets.
Gathered armfuls of memories and experiences
and nursed them carefully, like June wildflowers in
mason jars. With pencils tucked behind our ears,
we drafted blueprints and plans on errant scraps
of paper. We scribbled and erased. Got frustrated
and kicked door jambs. Cried into each other.
Learned from our mistakes. And planned again.

And together, we had engineered a marvel.

Oh, the magnificence.

A bridge.

A bridge, suspended safely over bays of wild, churning
waters, carefully crafted to withstand torrents and
tempests that would threaten us with devastation.

A bridge with gilded spires, constructed from our
pocketsful of visions and dreams, that peaked over
the clouds, gracefully suspended by powerful

cables. Cables were intricately woven together from a million moments of tender intimacy. Strands spun from moments of gentle hand squeezes and smiling pinky promises. From the joy and elation when we brought babies into the world together. From heartbreaking absences and the rawness of grief. Tender glances in the mirror. Scrawled love notes. Nights of vulnerability and moments of unabashed confidence. Forgiveness and trying, trying, trying again with all the hope we could muster.

A bridge to span from the shore of our humble beginnings and extend to the end of, well, forever.

We were safe, he and I.

Together forever, we said.

congratulations

I looked like a wax statue in the vicinity of a blow torch.

Hoping to cover the mountains of stress-induced acne on my lower jaw, I had applied liberal amounts of concealer and ill-matching foundation. To be frank, my overall makeup application (caked-on Cover Girl + heavy eyeliner, circa 2006) was mediocre at best. National Geographic mistook me for a Blobfish as the thick Kentucky humidity melted my makeup into the creases of my neck.

My naturally wavy hair succumbed to the curl that lies in wait at the base of my neck, and ringlets appeared under my la coiffure—the French twist I had spun that morning, held precariously by some White Rain wallpaper paste.

My mom, a talented seamstress, had sewn my dress in an effort to keep costs down and add a personal touch to my family's first wedding. To maintain the high standard of Mormon modesty, we had combined two wedding dress patterns into what I hoped would be a luxurious gown of pearl and chiffon. However, sewing the chiffon had proven challenging, even for my seamstress-inclined mother. The gown fell just above my knobby ankles, and the yoke along my back and shoulder blades was so large it could house a humpback. I could have very well smuggled several tiny humans or a truckload of cheeseburgers inside that oversized lining. Ultimately, the dress mash-up had failed miserably.

I felt like one of those cheeseburgers.
A melted, hideous cheeseburger.

Alas, in addition to our mini disasters, the florist
had forgotten that INDEED I had placed an
order for flowers; she discovered a tucked-away
invoice in a little dark place called the recycle
bin. She lacked any and all recollection that she
was supposed to have lively summer bouquets
to brighten up my mopey little ceremony.

The reception was simple and reminiscent of a
grandma's basement, partly because it was tasked
by a group of industrious Mormon women. Let me
be clear—there is no work ethic like a gaggle of fiery
Christian women. A church gymnasium held white
trellises decorated with silk flowers, and the busy
floral-print chairs from the foyer staggered the room.
Round tables dotted the floor, only minimally covering
the black basketball free throw lines. Silk gerbera
daisies floated in small vases of water while the
buffet line consisted of ham and cheese sandwiches,
fruit salsa, and tiny homemade butter mints.

The events were documented by an earnest, budding
photographer who shot the photos as a wedding
present sans digital documentation, the overexposed
35 mm film washing out features and blurring faces.
These poorly executed images of a mediocre,
un-whimsical day sat in boxes for years and were
marginally easy to throw away when my divorce came.

Happy wedding day.

the ugly

"We have had some happy times together,"
he said as we held hands one night.

I nodded, remembering the births of our girls,
date nights spent laughing together as we
learned how to love each other, how to grow
through grief and hurt on both parts.

We were babies when our relationship started,
having met and married in the span of twelve weeks.
We didn't know how to love the other and were
learning through trial and error how to navigate the
ugly parts of marriage that no one talked about.

I wouldn't patch or doctor the ugly parts to make them
more beautiful, to appear airbrushed or wrinkle-free.

I'll take the ugly, the flawed, the imperfect.

I'll keep things just as they were.

the maid's porn

He told me the maid did it.

The maid, he said, had come into our hotel
room, logged into his laptop, and looked
up numerous graphic porn sites.

Sincerity dripped from his slick, lubricated words,
which left oily stains on my impressionable mind.

And I believed him.

a conversation

you said
and
i said
and this side
and that

no
you're making that up
it didn't happen
the way you say

i never said that

yes, you did
i heard you

a carbonated conversation—
fizzy bubbles blurring
the recollections of
who said
what really happened:
when did i say that
why don't you listen to me

we push
and pull
and sing
and crow,
but can we really know
what lie
sandwiched

between the bread and butter
of our colloquy?

in the end
all i know
is what i felt
and what i said
and what you did
and what i did
and what we did
together

obviously, i trust
keen ears that hear
what i want to hear,
eyes that
reflect my own
burnished bias,
lips that flatter me
as i highlight and contour myself
in the very best light

and if my version
isn't your version,
then whose verse
holds veracity?

it must have been mine
or my own narrative is just that—
fiction,
fabricated in
faux fidelity

and to be honest,
i suppose i must ask—

did it really happen that way,
the way i say?

you say no.

is this how history
becomes
history?

abs

"Did you go to the gym today?" he
asked as I walked in the door.

"Yes, I went after preschool," I responded, dropping
heavy grocery bags onto the countertops. He met
me in the kitchen, and I leaned into him for a hug.

He held me for a moment, his hands lingering
at my midriff. He squeezed my stomach,
scarred by puckered stretch marks, and used
his fingers to jab me firmly in the core.

I tensed, embarrassed by the stretched
skin he held in his hands.

"See, you've got abs in there somewhere,"
he said. "You just need to find them."

I laughed.

I'm not sure why.

the outlier

i'm not a cheater, you say.
you play by the rules.

but the rules are skewed and
i don't know which ones to keep
which ones to forget
to look away
to ignore

do you keep the same set of rules as i
or do you keep your own?

you show your body to other women
but you don't show me

you say you admire me
but do you sacrifice for me

i am hidden
invisible
uncredited
back-burnered
an afterthought

our future is miraged
behind the past
you refuse to part with

you fear
being seen
by and with

the woman
you married

you are afraid because of me

i am short-changed
yet
i'm asking for the same amount

you are more a stranger to me now than
when we were strangers

if you don't want to tell people you have a wife,
don't have one.

stupid things he said to me

On climaxing: "Can you hurry up?"

After 3 years of marriage: "I just don't really find you attractive."

his[story] repeated

a cock
and a bull
concoct a story
manufactured to
please the cock,
and hide the smell of bull

shit,
who cares
it's his[story]
his truth in cock-colored glasses
crowing as he
bullies his way through delicate fidelity
careless as he strokes
his own ego
and manhandles
she + her + me + them
until it suits him

speaking of suits
what tales did you spin
to fabricate
the cheap pants
caught around your ankles?
didn't you read the tag?
caution: flammable

let me ask you,
do you lie
for fun

for games
to damn your neighbor
or to fuck with your wife,
but not in the way
she'd like to be fucked

anyway,
in the end
it's the cock
and bull story
that everyone
remembers.

condoms in his pockets

The news of his affair was only days old, its
stale scent lingering in our bed, crawling on
my skin, yellowing our years of intimacy.

He leaned against the piano, his arms
crossed casually in front of him.

I sat uncomfortably on our faux leather couch,
wishing I could press my face against its cool
surface as I listened to him detail the hidden
cash advances on our credit cards, the train rides
with condoms in his pockets, the disapproving
suitemates who could've said something, but
instead put on headphones and turned away.

He paused.

"You know, she reminds me a lot of you, actually,"
he said, looking up at me. He raised his eyebrows, a
sheepish smile flickering at the corners of his mouth.

I nodded slowly, involuntarily.

She.

She is like me? Or I am like her?

Then, who reminds him of whom? How can
he remember us if we are all the same?

Blurs of brunette, faceless women—tidy
transactional slips clocked in and out.

Just condoms in his pockets.

happiness

He left his phone at home that morning.

It's funny just what we remember.

I just couldn't run the phone to his office that day; I had school to teach, errands to run, girls to carpool, and musical practice that afternoon. Our predictable, busy life wasn't unhappy; we bloomed with routine. We had created a content situation full of schedules and duties and homemade dinners and frequent date nights.

I loved him. And he loved me.

I decided to text his best friend—with whom he had eternal running text commentary—to ask him to pass along the message that he would have to come and grab the phone himself.

I entered his familiar six-digit pin and pulled up his messages.

Ice filled my veins as I sat in shock, staring at proof memorialized in blue on a cracked iPhone screen.

The pictures. The words. The allusions. The promises.

We don't ever really see it coming.
Or do we?

Disbelief dropped into my stomach, a heavy stone tossed into a placid lake. Waves and ripples disrupted the previously smooth and glassy water, and with a hollow plunk, I'm caving in on myself under the weight and pressure of betrayal. I sink deeper, my lungs gasping for air as I struggle to breathe.

I might be drowning.

I think I'm drowning.

We were happy.
Weren't we happy?

Tears don't come yet.
They never do.

He had said it would never happen again.

I think I knew.

Things had been too good.
Too simple.
Too happy.
Too easy.

Maybe I know I knew.

And the secret I had shoved somewhere in the attic behind forgiveness and healing began rapping heavily on my heart. The truth I had desperately been trying to put behind me, the truth that no one could really understand. It couldn't be tucked away, hidden behind smiling family photos and goodbye kisses.

I feared happiness.

For years and years, happiness had brought me grief. Happiness had slowly become entangled with deceit. Had tricked me and had made me feel stupid.

Happiness had drowned me before.

But still, after years of deceptive happiness, I stubbornly resisted the façade, buying into the idea that we *were* happy. We HAD to be happy. We had worked so hard to develop our equation of assurance, our own calculation of contentment.

We. Were. Happy.

Dammit.

My resistance bred naivete and ignorance. The red flags were still only a shade of pink, all explainable and patched with patronizing platitudes. I hid his glaring inconsistencies behind Instagram posts of our happy family and minimized his duplicity with blinders. I believed his lies. I believed them so deeply because if I could just *give him all I was*, wouldn't that mean we would be happy?

His charm blossomed for it.

He was so careful. His cunning charisma smoothed over my confusion and fear— a manipulated measure of calm, grooming me for happiness in exchange for trickery and deceit. He knew how to invest in me, how to trade me for chump change, how to master the appearance I so desperately wanted.

He knew the precarious balance that offered his freedom: Happiness at home allowed for his protected time alone.

Well, not alone.

It just wasn't with me.

———————————

He left his phone at home that day.

I'm still afraid to feel happy.

the email that changed things

From: Kiera
Sent: Tuesday, March 27, 2018 8:17 AM
To: Him
Subject: Re: word?

Me: You left your phone here on the couch

Him: Yea I know. I'm going to go home
      and pick it up in a min.

Me: You're a real asshole by the way. I can't
      believe you talk about other girls like the
      way you and your friend are. It's so rude and
      disrespectful and I can't believe you do that.

Him: I warned you about our conversations

Me: Not about real girls and wanting to have
      sex with them. You're a real prick.

Him: Then don't read my messages

Me: Then don't do it.

broken bridges, part II

I feel sickening thuds as the cables that tether
me to safety rip from their bolted anchors.

The once-secure cables arc violently in the air. The
strands of interlacing tenderness and memories
begin to unravel, to fray. The strands that we
had spent a million moments weaving together.
How it had chafed and calloused our hands.

How fast they were coming undone.

No longer anchored, the golden spires tilt
precariously. No. Our dreams. Our pocketsful
of magic and wonder. Our love, so deeply
embedded in our blueprints, our fine-tuned
plans. Our carefully cared-for hopes.

We are collapsing.

The vision of our future begins to crumble,
to fall, to collapse, raining down pieces
of broken, devastating grandeur.

Pieces of us.

Of me.

No.

I reach out to grab our memories and tender pieces
of my heart, but they're falling too fast. My arms
are laden with experiences that have lost their

luster, but I cling and cling to them, echoes of our rich, golden past. I can't. I can't let them go. Why can't I save them all? Each scrap is too precious to leave behind but too heavy to carry on my own.

I call to him, my breathing ragged.

"But our dreams! Our future! Please. Help me. Help me hold them," I beg.

He doesn't look back.

I look around, desperately. Aching for something familiar to pull me to safety. To tether me. The cables lie abandoned, the golden towers mere semblances of their former grandeur. There is nothing left.

Nothing holds the bridge anymore.

Nothing holds me anymore.

And I fall.

a thursday

A day for the books.

He brought me a bag of peanut butter M&Ms and my favorite soda, a fountain Diet Coke with easy ice and sugar-free coconut syrup.

I looked at him, confused. His eyes were tender as they met mine. My resolve for emotional control began to dissolve under his sincerity.

"I know it's been a hard day," he said, almost compassionately.

It had been.

He'd asked me for a divorce.

I remember

I remember
a Sunday morning
in the bed we shared.

He told me he just couldn't

he couldn't love me.
he couldn't grow.
he couldn't stay.

not anymore.

I remember

he looked at me,
his blue eyes filled
as he held my hand

one last time.

"This is it?" I asked.

"This is it," he said.

I remember

we wept
we couldn't be
what we could be.

We broke

an eternal
collapse.

And yet

I knew
peace.

another one

Another woman.

FUCK. How many was it, now? Five? Six?

Anger swept through my body — a hot, tortuous fire consuming a drought-ridden forest.

"I'm going to report this, and you'll lose your job," I spat at him. I couldn't summon an ounce more of understanding, of patience. We hadn't even told our kids yet about the pending divorce. I was still reeling under its weight.

Another woman already?

The news was too heavy to shore, and I opened the front door to the chilly May night and sat on the cool, concrete steps.

His elongated shadow soon darkened the steps as he stood in the doorway.

"Think rationally about this, Kiera. If I lose my job, I can't support you and the girls. It's not the smart thing to do. You know that." His voice was controlled and calculated.

I ached at his words, my stomach roiling in anxiety and fear at my blank, penniless future, dependent on him to care for us as callously as he had done in our marriage.

An impossible decision in an impossible moment.

And I let him win again.

to fall out of love

I knew I'd fallen out of love
when I didn't miss his touch.

I knew I'd fallen out of love
when the distance in our bed grew apart
by inches and stomachaches,
headaches and mismatched bedtimes.

I knew I'd fallen out of love
when I listened to him debate
about staying or leaving,
not because he loved me, no—
how could he leave a wife who loved him?

I knew I'd fallen out of love
when I took off the old rosy lenses
and really saw him for the first time—
I had to close my eyes at his ugliness.

I knew I'd fallen out of love
when he asked me months after the divorce
if I wanted to try again,
and I said no.

I knew I'd fallen out of love
when I gave myself permission
to stop loving him.

God, I love
not loving him.

permission

i am allowed
to be something
to want something
to need something
to do something

and i am allowed to place claim on that thing—

whether it's something
or nothing
or anything
or everything—

and i can say, "this is how i feel" and
i am allowed to feel that—

i am allowed to
need
want
see
become

more
or
less
than i am

and i give myself permission to make mistakes—
and i will not feel your shame
at your inability to do the same
and will not flinch when you
cast that first stone

sticks and stones won't break my bones
because
your power is lost

i am allowed to think and do and be
without fear of you
without fear of your fear
without fear of what you can do
because you can't control me

you are chained by the need to be
validated
esteemed
prickled with pomp and circumstance

i'm free

of you

the day we told the girls

a note in my phone

May 2018

We have some important big changes
that we are having in our family.

This might seem scary and sad and different
and that's okay. It will take a lot of courage and
time to be able to adapt to these changes.

We love you so much. So much. You are the ONLY
thing we think about when we make decisions. We
love you beyond the moon and back. And we want
you to always remember how much we love you.

Mom loves each of you. Dad loves each of you.
And mom and dad have worked really hard to love
each other, but sometimes that love changes and
it's hard to stay married together. So even though
we still love each other in a special Mom and Dad
way, we aren't going to be married anymore.

Mom and Dad are getting what's called a divorce.
This may seem like a big scary word. But it
means that Dad will still love you so so so much
and Mom will still love you so so so much, but
Dad will move out to a new place and live there.
Mom and Dad won't live together anymore.

But guess what?

Mom still loves you. Dad still loves you. And Mom and Dad still love each other in a friend way. But we aren't going to be married anymore.

Do you understand what this means?
Do you have questions?

We are going to still both be at recitals and the musical and birthdays and celebrations because that's important to us to be together to celebrate you guys.

It's going to be hard. You're not going to be able to see your dad as much as you do now, but when you do see him, you still should run up to him and give him big, big, big hugs like you do now!! He wants to still spend as much time with you, so when I need to go to meetings and things, he is going to watch you and will take you places. Once he gets a new apartment, you get to spend the night at his house and spend weekends with him.

This does not and will not ever change his love for you. Or mine! We are always here to support you and love you and give you everything you need.

But even though we are friends, we aren't going to ever get married to each other again.

We might have some changes—we might need to move houses and move schools to fit the changes in our life, but we will find new friends and a support system that measures up to our new life of loving you together, but separately.

We still love you forever.

leftovers

He didn't tell me they were coming.

I stood frozen in the doorway in a stained, yellow t-shirt as his friends, who were also my friends, walked past me in my entryway. They wore sneakers and empathic glances, and I watched them gather his items from our home and load them into the obscene U-Haul parked awkwardly in my steep driveway.

He hurried them into the bedroom we had shared, a sacred space now tainted with stains of infidelity. He pointed and gave directions as they unscrewed the heavy bed frame, threw the pieces over their shoulders, and carried away the bed we had lain in for many years, the bed in which widening space had consumed our final months. In fifteen minutes, he had erased the intimacy from what was once our beautiful bedroom. Our marriage was reduced to a dusty outline on carpeted floors.

He left the photo of us in beachside Monterey for me to remove from the wall.

Our friends carried away the couches, the ones chosen carefully to fit Sunday afternoon naps and snuggles from tiny babes. These couches had held deep conversations and sat visitors at holiday parties; errant pieces of popcorn fell from underneath cushions, leftover from late-night movies.

They took the new washer and dryer I had installed, his dresser full of clothes, and his tools from the garage—his gifts from Christmases and birthdays.

He took what he wanted and left the rest.

He had removed himself so callously from our home, leaving the leftovers for me to discard.

I took down the family pictures that stared at me from the stairwell, wept over photos of new babies and a long-past wedding, threw away romantic mementos tucked in boxes, donated items from a religion discarded, and shredded files of plans for our future.

How curious that twelve years lived together could vanish in the course of one afternoon.

the canvas

The rain poured outside, filling gutters and
window wells and sending torrents of water
down the hill in front of my house.

I lugged the giant canvas portrait outside.

A photo of the two of us, taken in Monterey,
California, as we laughed and tried to balance
precariously over tide pools and crashing waves.

It had hung above our bed.

I placed it inside the overfilled trash can, which was
waiting at the end of the driveway for pickup.

A car drove by, slowed down, and rolled
to a stop in front of my house.

"Oh, Kiera," said the driver. "I know it's hard
right now, but you might want to keep
that photo, just for the memories."

I turned and walked away.

a letter

My dear girl,

One day, your grief will subside.
One day, your pain will not sit on a
pedestal, too tender to touch.

One day.

But for now, feel the breaking of your heart.
Let the fractures shatter within you, sending
shrapnel into unprotected self-worth. Let every
splintered piece echo as it falls free from the web
of deception in which you were entangled.

The truth has set you painfully, terrifyingly free.

You will feel the burden of grief many years from
now, even after you have let in the grace, after
you have let self-compassion flow through your
veins. You will feel the twinges of loss on auburn
fall days and during the pain of loneliness.

But I promise you. I promise me.

See, I'm a few years wiser,
and you are growing infinitely, irrevocably stronger.
You will stand on boulders that previously seemed
impassable.
The wind, the water, the air will envy
the peace you will let live in you.

It might not matter today
or tomorrow
or the nights that feel heavy and alone.

But one day, your daughter will say, "I
want to be as strong as my mom."

And you'll remember a divine sort of memory, an
identity that you once felt long ago:
"I matter."

I'll sit with you, through the rubble of grief
and the rebuilding of your heart.

Love,
The very same girl

stupid things he said to me

During divorce mediation: "When do you think you'll get remarried?"

the smile

I find myself blocked.

My recently broken heart is still pumping, my nervous system fully responsive. I trace my hands over my skin simply to feel physical contact.

I am still alive.

Yet, my emotions are numb. Burned. Deadened by fatigue and the still-raw memories of abandonment.

Head up. I face others with illicit strength—
stolen from where? From whom did I
siphon the strength that carries me?

Invisible power gathers my beating heart
into a too-tight grip as it pumps blood
ruthlessly through my veins: whywhy whywhy
whywhy whywhy did this happen?

And I hear **them**. **They**, the invisible keepers
of wisdom and convention. **They**, the
ones who know how to traverse the pain
that threatens to turn me to dust.

"Let it go," they say.

How can they know what I feel or how I feel it?

they don't they don't they don't.

"Have faith," they chant.

I can't. I don't. I won't.

WHYWHYWHYWHY can't I feel the faith that
so peacefully guides them down the strait?

Why must I fight to not be buried in bitterness?

I sneak through the brambles of hurt, hiding deep
gashes and gouges from branches that whip and
thorns that bury. No doubt, they claim, my wounds will
be healed by my faith—the same faith that evades. I
come out on the other side smiling at my good fortune,
at my past redeemed.

But my smile doesn't touch my eyes.

whittling

I sat in the office of a religious counselor,
fuming at the memories of betrayal and
infidelity, only two weeks young.

He looked at me from behind his
builder-grade oak veneer desk, his face
compassionate, his words gentle.

"It's okay to be angry. Anger is a part of healing,"
he explained. "Anger is part of forgiveness."

"I just don't know if I want to forgive him," I said.

"I know it seems that way now. But this is your
eternal family at stake," he said. "Don't worry;
we'll keep whittling down your sharp edges."

My sharp edges?

Dear sir: There's no knife you can wield that will
be permitted to smooth down any part of me.

I've let too many carve me into the shapes of
their liking; any future sculpting is mine.

I've earned the sharp juts and rough calluses
that catch on soft skin and silk. I don't want to
be smoothed out with the sandpaper of prayers
and platitudes, but instead, I'd like to keep my
edges as a reminder of the bravery that has led

me from battle to battle. I want the tenacity of
perseverance; I'd like the sharp edges to show.

No, sir.

You'll not whittle anything down.

I'll stay this way.

part 3:
disrobing motherhood

"I am prouder of my years as a single mother than of any other time of my life."
J.K. Rowling

stupid things people have said to me

"It's not that fucking hard to be a mom, Kiera. Stop fucking it up."

and she ran, part 1

Fuck.

Fuck, fuck, fuck.

The frigidity of this particular December morning blew in through the open van windows as I rounded the corner, clipping the curb.

I parked hastily, threw the door shut behind me, and took off across the icy asphalt. My breath leached out of me in the early morning cold like cigarette smoke, and I kept pace to get hold of my daughter, bolting through yards and down the streets.

I was chasing her.

and she ran, part 2

Did I know, at the onset of motherhood,
the complexity of raising a child?

That joy and love link arms with grief and sorrow? That
pride and peace juxtapose with shame and guilt?

It's painful. Heavy. It weighs on us.
Burns us. Knocks us down.

I had absolutely no idea what exactly a mother
would do to keep her daughter safe.

The things I would do for her.

So I ran after her.

That morning, a fit of fear and anxiety triggered the
flight response in my daughter's brain, and she had
to escape. She screamed and threatened, and as
I tried to safely pull the car over, she jumped out,
leaving her coat and backpack on the front seat.

And she ran.

Running away wasn't abnormal for
her, but this time was different.

Perhaps it was the earliness of the hour for
how quickly her emotions had accelerated.

Perhaps it was that I didn't know what she needed.

Perhaps it was that I didn't know how to love her the way she needed to be loved.

But this baby of mine.

This girl.

For whatever reason, she was burning, seething with and blinded by a nameless, reckless rage. A rage that masked internal fear, terror, and suffering inside her carefully protected heart.

Her bruised heart.
Her broken heart.

In moments, I was flanked by other adults, chasing her by car and on foot down streets and around corners. In the panic of the moment, a seemingly well-intentioned parent called the police, and two uniformed officers followed carefully behind me.

No, this is all wrong, I thought.

I caught up to her.

She was winded, clutching at her sides. She was combustible, her face red with cold. A misstep, a careless word or faux sincerity would detonate her— a dangerous battlefield we stood upon.

I approached her.

She bristled.

I said her name.

Her bright hazel eyes glared at me, then glanced frantically at the adults surrounding her. A bus stop full of teenagers gawked at her, mere feet away from where we stood. She wrapped her arms around her body, protecting herself, as realization flooded her.

This unwanted attention spotlighted her,
held her captive in its garish beam.

The blindness and furious adrenaline that
had made her run began to dissipate, and she
stood frozen by the cold, her heart bearing
the wounds and burdens of her actions.

"Mom!" she cried out, pleading.

I was there.

I do a million things wrong every day.

But I was there.

I feel tired

The kind of tired that carves wrinkles into chasms and deepens dark shadows lurking under heavy eyes.

Fiery, brooding emotions test my patience
and tolerance, and I fear implosions
under the pressure of fatigue.

I am dangerously combustible over trivialities.

The air around me is static with the
electricity of movement.

But me?

I'm the Tin Man, grayscale and immobile, suspended motionless in a prism of colorful blurs.

The one with a tired heart in desperate need of repair.

bowls of parmesan

I swore. Loudly. A volcanic eruption of words
began as a tremor and exploded into fiery fury.

An absolutely disgusting mess.

Sweat dripped from my forehead as I lay on the
floor, trying to squeeze my arm as far as it would go
underneath my bed frame to reach the, oh this is
gonna be good, overflowing *landfill* of trash and dirty
dishes I had just discovered hidden in the shadows.

Marie Kondo, just fair warning, you
are not invited to my house.

The soundtrack of my life changed from
ominous instrumentals to gangster rap with DMX
screaming prophetic lyrics of "Y'ALL GON MAKE
ME LOSE MY MIND, UP IN HERE, UP IN HERE."

I bravely reached into the abyss and grabbed fruit
snack wrappers, Otter Pop plastics, empty Ritz
cracker sleeves, and a bag of tortilla chips (minus the
chips) with my fingertips. I pulled out seven bowls
with Frosted Flakes remnants and spoons glued to
the rubbery sugar milk combo dried at the bottom.
Cups tinted with dried colors of Crystal Light flavors.
*What humanless creatures am I raising?? Corn dog
sticks?? Marie Callender's Chicken Pot Pie tins?*

And… What?

bowls. of. parmesan.

Yes. Yep. Definitely what you think. Desiccated, dried, crumbly parmesan. Like, the kind you get in a clear canister above the pasta; the kind that costs roughly $1.79. Come on, you know. You know.

Bowls of it. Under my bed. Complete with plastic spoons for what? Etiquette's sake?

Apparently, as my kids are sneaking YouTube videos in the morning when they are supposed to be making dioramas of solar systems and studying fossils or something (and they PINKY PROMISED THEY WOULD—oh, the BETRAYAL), they decided that this was also a great time to scarf down bowls of parmesan? THAT IS THEIR CONTRABAND?

I don't get it.

When I was a kid and money was super tight, and because my mom locked up all the field trip snacks into a closet (which is just some insight into definitely also why I had weird food issues for twenty years), we didn't go around and say, "Oh boy, you know what sounds just delish? A BOWL OF PARMESAN CHEESE." We made French toast at midnight while opening all the windows so Mom and Dad wouldn't notice. Like NORMAL PEOPLE.

So, to me, this begs several questions.

First off, obviously, which one of them is going to pay me back for the $1.79, but also, why are my kids so weird?

Next, where did they get the idea that I would never find the 24 thousand cheap plastic bowls stowed away under my bed?

Lastly, and probably most importantly, how are they eating it without accidentally coughing it up into their lungs and then spewing forth the remnants? Oh hell, now I know why my bed was covered with towels and water that day. Those little parmesan addicts.

So, the moral of this story is that not one human under the age of 37 and 11 months is allowed in my bedroom ever again.

The end.

enough

I hate dinner.

It would take too long to explain the complexities of my twisty brain, but suffice it to say, I loathe the task of planning for and cooking dinner.

So sometimes (read: uhhlotttt), my kids get microwaved quesadillas and how-old-are-these-leftover-tacos? to eat when the hunger + anger combo hits about 6:00 p.m.

And when the weather is perfectly temperate and the dining room table is cluttered, we take our mediocre dinner out to our messy, piecemeal front porch.

And we sit together and eat dinner in the sunset while Scarlett makes whistles out of straws.

No hoopla. No fighting. No deep conversations. No nutrition.

Damn.

I love when we can feel the beauty of being enough.

magic and anarchy

"Mom. Why don't you ever play with us?"

I froze as I lay on the concrete floor of the garage, shop-vacuuming decrepit corners of old spiderwebs and dead pill bugs. My skin and clothes were layered thick with dust and grime and abandoned sidewalk chalk that had been crushed by the wheels of my minivan.

Hmm, I thought in that quick millisecond that precedes a response. *Do I respond with patience and understanding or anger?*

"DUDE," I started. (A note for future interactions: If it starts this way, probably back way the hell up.)

"Momma, I just want to play frisbee with you."

Cue all the emotions. The melty heart, the brutal mom guilt, the creaky old body that was on the floor all day (now running after errant frisbees), the not getting to check off my tidy to-do list, and the frisbee-then-sidewalk-chalk-then hopscotch-then-batting-practice-then-"Oh how about mac and cheese for dinner?"

It's all there. Every contiguous emotion, from elation to sorrow, all wrapped up in a tidy little package of "Mom, why don't you ever play with us?"

And guess what? I'm not going to tell you to find joy in the journey. I'm not going to tell you to "make the memories" when they are small. I'm not going to force-feed guilt into your needs or wants as you check off to-do lists, develop talents and hobbies, or learn to better yourself. There's no way I'm going to see you there in survival mode and ask, "Um, ew, okay, can you please do more than what you are capable of giving?"

Nope.

I'm going to tell you that I DO NOT KNOW HOW TO BE THE BEST MOM TO MY KIDS, and I have a rather healthy addiction to Milk Duds and Coke Zero to prove it.

Some days will be magical, and some days will be anarchy.

But, our love matters.

We matter.

slow down

We stayed at home.

A wince-worthy CV axle in-shop repair
made for an active recovery afternoon.

No gas station runs for an afternoon pick-me-up or
rushing to find charged tablets for the CrossFit kids'
room. No "be-back-in-five-minutes" after I realized
that we were out of milk, bread, and Eggo waffles.

Obligatory time off.

We slowed down like the cogs of a
clock that grind slowly to a halt.

We stopped rushing and felt the stillness instead.

We spent the afternoon on the cold concrete,
doodling with chalk and graffitiing the sidewalk
with typefaces and bright colors to urge spring
out of its hesitant crocus buds. We played
hopscotch and made German pancakes and
threw away clutter. We broke bread and cracked
smiles. We shared the happy parts and the sad
parts and cleaned dishes and swept floors.

I normalize the rush, for what? The fierce
competition of doing more or being more? My
mind fills daily with rush-hour traffic as I face
heady deadlines of "must-do" and "must-be."

I glorify the busy. I canonize my to-do list. I worship time in constant productivity.

Until I recite the glorious charge of "slow the hell down" over and over and over again and watch as the days grow longer and the faces of my babies stay baby a little longer.

It's uncomfortable to decelerate.

It's painful to pause.

I can only assume that when the $641 is paid and the keys are back in the ignition, I'll once again taxi until only fumes remain.

But the chalk, a relic of obligatory pauses, stays dusty on the sidewalk.

legos

I'm sitting at the dining room table, quietly picking at my scrambled eggs on wheat toast.

Wednesdays are long days. I don't feel much like talking. Instead, I watch my girls, who are sitting at the counter on too-tall barstools, laughing and indulging in make-believe.

They're listening to the Frozen 2 soundtrack while putting together a Frozen Lego set Scarlett earned for listening (it only took 7 million centuries).

The counter is littered with cereal bags, excess cornstarch from afternoon oobleck creations, paper plates with remnants of macaroni and cheese, and empty boxes just waiting for someone to toss them in the recycle bin. And a pillow (I'm confused by that one).

Blankets and watercolor pictures and spare mittens and more Legos pepper the floor.

The trash needs to be taken out.

I start to spiral. To fall into victimhood. To let the "never enoughs" lay bricks and mortar on my chest, inhibiting my breaths. I'm imploding inside. Shattering.

Nothing is clean.

Nothing is presentable.

Nothing is perfect.

Suddenly, my two oldest daughters turn to me, wave a Lego creation, and shout enthusiastically, "Mom! Look what Scarlett did! She did it all by herself!"

Scarlett blushes and beams. Her sisters squeeze her.

Nobody move. Nobody change. Nobody grow. Freeze this moment, this mess, this beauty, these tears.

Oh.

Everything is PERFECT.

I can see now.

the nameless woman

The sound of vomiting interrupted Idina Menzel's mezzo-soprano belting from the van stereo.

I froze.

Stuck in the confines of the driver's seat, I whipped my head around to see my four-year-old losing her lunch inside our family Honda, which was parked in the rear of a Walmart parking lot. Nestled gently against my chest was my brand-new baby, nursing contentedly while we waited for my mom, who was picking up necessary postpartum essentials like generic stool softeners and, hopefully, a LOT of alcohol. I mean, baby wipes.

I was trapped in a vacuum, stuck by the incessant suckling of a needy infant and also the sour vomit smell that wafted through the vent system.

"Mommy!" Her voice warbled with that sort of panicky, wavery quivering associated only with highly inopportune sickness. "I have to go to the bathroom!"

Oh, shit.

I cut the newborn off of her food supply, pulled up my v-neck as she wailed like the needy, whiny little baby she was, and threw open the front door.

Early February frost tickled my nose as I wrapped my baby in my coat, grabbed my bilious preschooler, and commanded my kindergartner to follow me.

We ran like the dickens.

No, sorry. That's not at all accurate. They ran. I hobbled like a wonky, overweight goose. (My last baby was a natural delivery. Shut up.)

Anyway, we "ran."

The store's automatic doors slid open, and I sent my oldest (six—she was six, oh hell) to find her tiny Nana in the giant, overfilled Walmart. I saw her run up the aisles like a fierce bloodhound.

"We'll be in the bathroom!" I shouted after her, grateful at this moment for her fiery defiance, a trait I usually cursed.

Holding my new baby in one arm, I pulled on the hand of my four-year-old, whose cheeks were pale and whose chubby legs couldn't keep up with my hobbling, episiotomied six-foot frame.

She is gonna blow, I thought.

The three of us hoofed into the nearly vacant bathroom, and my sick babe disappeared behind a stall door. I tried to catch my breath while rocking a startled, hungry baby in my arms.

"Mom!" my sick babe shouted from the stall. "I'm going to throw up AND go to the bathroom!"

The milliseconds hung heavy in the air.

These nano-moments are where we face our heaviest reaction receptors. Decision-making kicks in. We fight. We run. Or we freeze.

One of my arms reached for the stall door while the other tucked the wailing baby closer to me.

"Mom! Help me!" cried the sick one who had started this whole mess. I still hold a grudge.

I looked around frantically for a nearby changing station. Nothing. A countertop. A cart! An emergency "my kid is going all 'double-headed dragon' on me" kit. Anything. But there was nothing.

Except the floor.

The floor, stained with urine and feces, trod on by a million shoe soles and the bacteria-filled head of an old mop.

I'm going to have to lay my baby on the floor, I thought, coming to terms with the vulgarity of this decision.

My baby. Tiny. New. Innocent. Uncompromised and healthy. Perinatal emotions began to compromise me. I felt the heat of panic enter my heart.

I knelt down.

"I can help!" a voice called out. Stuck in my momentary anxiety, I hadn't noticed another person in the bathroom. "I'm a grandma! I can hold your baby. I can help!"

I looked up at her, this nameless
woman, as she came into focus.

For one incredibly long, eternal second, I took in
her kind smile. I saw her hurry to me. I watched
her demeanor as she reached towards me.
I saw compassion in her eyes, concern and
tenderness in the lines on her face. I saw a flicker
of mutual understanding, of trust between two
women who believed the utter best in each
other during that impossible moment.

My instinct said yes.

My gut said yes.

My heart said yes.

And I handed my brand-new baby to a
stranger, a nameless woman, in the filthy,
unfamiliar Walmart bathroom.

As I turned to open the stall door, I saw her rocking
my newborn, rhythmically swaying back and
forth to calm her. She cooed at my babe. I heard
her sing a little ditty that only grandmas know.

I knelt on the bathroom floor and held my
scared preschooler as she cried into me.

I don't remember much after that.

A small story, perhaps.

How is it, though, that this small story fills my
eyes with grateful tears, and a lump forms

in my throat at the thought of this nameless
woman who saw a young-ish, scared mother
one morning while out on her errands?

A nameless woman who must've felt
my palpable panic in the air.

A nameless woman who could've ignored
my plight and left me to fend for myself.

Now, I'm an intelligent woman and no stranger to
the resilience of making my own way. Hindsight
and the wisdom of experience remind me that, no,
life would not have ended in that moment if I'd had
to set my brand-new baby on the Walmart floor.

But then I'd not have this story to
tell of this nameless woman.

The nameless woman who shared the
love of a compassionate God and who
stitched an eternal moment of empathy and
humanity into the tapestry of my heart.

If I could be anything in this world,

I'd be a nameless woman.

we need the dark

My daughter and I spoke tonight of fears and angsts, of anxieties that might seem silly to other children.

But I fear the dark, too, my girl.

The darkness I fear is not the night's spindly shadows distorted through window blinds, stretched along midnight walls, but is instead the darkness of hearts and minds, the blindness of power and control.

Too, we are humans: raw, aching, real, and irrevocably flawed. Burdened by grief and inadequacies, we darken our own eyes with the falsity that we will never again see the sun.

But the night does not last forever, darling.

We need the dark, you know. We need the cyclical power of change, of growth, of dissent and antagonism. We learn to desperately fuel our own wicks to combat the saturating, oncoming darkness.

She and I spoke of light tonight.

Light, my love, is merely the absence of darkness. Light is brilliance, yes, but also subtle and safe—a warm glow that comforts our hearts and repels the shadows that squirm and slink in our cognitive alleyways, uninvited to the safety within.

Your compassion is light. Your kindness is light. Your grace is light.

You are my light, too, my girl.

the blizzard

Snow fell that night in Colorado Springs, stranding my minivan in a tall, nearly inaccessible snowbank.

I stared through my ninth-floor hotel window, suffocating from anxiety.

A blizzard warning had been issued over Thanksgiving week for the central Colorado area, with more to come, and we were stuck in its drifts in the parking lot at the Great Wolf Lodge.

My mind whirled.

My girls and I had a ten-hour home-bound drive through the Rockies, and the snow had hit the tallest peaks and had shut down passage westbound on I-70 due to accidents and icy roads. Our hotel time had expired, and the contents of my depleting bank account begged me to come up with a feasible, inexpensive solution.

And I hate, hate, hate driving in the snow.

Trying not to panic, I flipped through a mental Rolodex of solutions. Fear set in, and I felt angry for having to make this decision on my own. Parenting is not so simply a series of split-second decisions. Evaluate. Act. Evaluate. Act. Rinse and repeat.

Mere moments had passed.

"Mom? Are you okay?" whispered my oldest, seeing my distraught face.

"Yes," I lied. I was going to find a way to safely outdrive the snow.

We rushed downstairs to dig the van out of its accumulating blanket of snow and hurriedly threw bags into the trunk. The girls clung nervously to souvenirs, pulled blankets up to their chins, and quietly soothed each other with gentle touches. We crept into a nearby QT gas station, loaded up with hot chocolate, donuts, egg sandwiches, and energy drinks, and watched as the snow fell quickly.

The compacted roads had turned to ice. Deep fog blocked my visibility as we offered a quick prayer for safety, gathered courage, and drove northbound.

My hastily formed plan began with driving through the burgeoning storm in centralized Denver. We could drive north to Cheyenne, about 3 hours away from our starting point, and head westbound on I-80 through Wyoming and into Salt Lake City.

This plan was rife with inconsistencies and very few contingencies. As we drove north, traffic on I-25 northbound to Cheyenne crawled to a dead stop outside of Denver.

We waited. And waited.

"Mom, when are we going to be there?" asked my then four-year-old.

I didn't know what to say. Placating and soothing troubled hearts felt out of my ability. Who would soothe mine? Fear quickened my heartbeat, and I felt helpless. I had no answers and less than a half a tank of gas.

"I'm trying to get us home safely, baby," I replied.

The snow hadn't stopped falling.

The car was quiet.

Snowplows passed us on the shoulder of the road, and soon, we held a steady 35 mph pace as we trudged north of Denver. I whispered a silent prayer of thanks to the universe and white-knuckled the steering wheel.

The falling snow began to lighten, dropping only moderately. The highway traction had improved, and we were moving steadily to Cheyenne. We plodded on.

"Mom?"

My oldest daughter's voice broke through my hunched-over, hyper-focused reverie. I stretched my shoulders and rolled my neck around.

"Mom, it's getting hard to see out the windows."

In my hyper-focus, I hadn't noticed the build-up of road sludge spattering the windshield. I turned on the windshield fluid and set the wipers to automatically clear the dinginess away.

The windshield wipers smeared mud
and gray slush in front of me.

I couldn't see out of the windshield.

I tried again, pumping vigorously to get fluid from
the lines. No fluid. The wipers continued to streak
the windows with darkness. I couldn't see the
road. I couldn't see cars. I couldn't see anything.

"Shit!" I yelled. I hunched over and peeked out
of the windshield through a small clearing on
the glass in order to find an exit and turn off.

The girls, shocked at hearing me lose my
composure, whimpered with fear.

"It's okay, babies," I said. "I just have to fix this."
Carefully, I pulled off onto an exit and found an old
gas station, nearly abandoned because of the storm.
I wrapped my coat around me, stepped outside
in the bitter wind and opened the hood, popping
off the top of the wiper fluid funnel. Wiper fluid
sloshed inside the tube, filling it to its capacity.

I didn't understand.

I stood in the cold, feeling numbness creep into
my fingertips. Why isn't it working? I grabbed
the gas station-provided squeegee and
cleaned the mud off the window. Naivete and
ignorance flirted with each other: *Maybe that's
it. Maybe it was just too dirty. Maybe it's fine.*

I got back into the car and tried the fluid again. Nothing. Swearing loudly, I slammed my hands against the steering wheel.

"It's probably frozen," offered the only other pump neighbor. "It will freeze overnight here."

I checked the GPS. Forty miles outside of Cheyenne. The weather radar showed that the snow had lightened considerably in northern Colorado.

I took a chance. We drove north.

Spirits were improving in the van; fear had been replaced with laughter and silliness. Confidence returned. We jammed out to songs from Spotify playlists. We belted out Disney ballads and played quintessential road trip games. The lack of wiper fluid became a running joke as we made obligatory stops to wipe down windows and grab overpriced, non-boring snacks.

Timid peace crept into my veins.

Be careful, it cautioned.

We were approaching both Cheyenne and dinner time. The snow had thickened, and large flakes were blanketing the windshield. As I debated stopping for dinner in Cheyenne or driving through to make up for lost time, we drove underneath a road conditions sign glaring in the developing darkness.

I-80 CLOSED WESTBOUND, it warned.

All freeways heading into Utah had been shut down because of the storm.

We were stranded just outside of Cheyenne.

Fear jolted through me. I eyed the westbound freeway. They had shut the snow gates, restricting all travel. Vehicles were being rerouted to Cheyenne to wait out the storm until the gates reopened. The city, usually electric with movement, was a sleepy ghost town. Storefronts were darkened, the snowy roads empty. I pulled into a motel parking lot and sat, stunned.

The girls' faces froze, the twinkles in their eyes and smiles vanishing completely, and they sat quietly as I rested my head on the steering wheel.

"Stay in the car," I ordered them. "Lock the door." I jumped out of the van, heard the doors lock behind me, and walked inside the motel with a faux bravery. A genial, middle-aged woman greeted me. Her Wyoming drawl was thick but not unkind.

"Can you tell me anything about the interstate?" I pleaded, after we had exchanged pleasantries. "When will it be open again?"

She looked at me pityingly.

"Girl," she replied. "This storm is supposed to go on for the rest of the week. It's not opening tonight or tomorrow or any time soon."

My head spun. I felt the instinct to curl up and let the weight of tears unburden themselves from my chest.

I glanced outside and saw three faces staring back at me, and I booked an inexpensive room for the night.

The girls watched mindless television shows with generic audience laugh tracks while I laid on the cardboard box masquerading as a bed. Gourmet vending machines provided our nutrition that evening with a spread of pepperoni hot pockets and bags of Cheetos and Sun Chips. Everyone shared a snack-size pack of Golden Oreos while I brainstormed and waffled and weaved in and out of ideas.

Around 9:30 that night, I tucked my girls into bed, promising insincerities of having clear heads and a game plan in the morning. I laid down next to my youngest and watched the Exit sign flicker in the darkened room.

Go back to Denver.

I froze.

A firm, powerful instinct struck me, plunging me into icy clarity. I sat up, looking over at my girls' sleepy faces reflected in the fluorescent glare of a dim television screen. Grabbing my phone, I hesitantly checked road conditions, hoping that this urgent prompting was a figment of my anxiety and that there was no way in actual hell it would be safe to travel southbound in the middle of the night.

Dammit.

Roads to Denver were plowed and clear. Snow had paused for enough time to let all of Colorado breathe. I-70 westbound was also open, requiring tire chains to navigate the icy roads, but open. By early morning, the traffic bosses promised, the pass through the Rockies would be free to travel sub-chain—but only for a few hours. This pause in inclement weather wouldn't last very long. Dangerous storms loomed ahead.

Go back to Denver now.

I listened.

After 3+ hours braving the icy roads and storms without wiper fluid and finding a soft place to land, we scrapped it all. Without explanation, I jumped out of bed and roused resistant, heavy-eyed babes.

"Come on, babes. We're trying this again."

Within minutes, four pajama-clad girls loaded in a tired Honda Odyssey, heading south to Denver.

A certain fragility and respect commanded the climate of the car as we drove back to Denver, the weather anticlimactic at best. Time passed quickly, and we stopped at a local Marriott for the night, whose front desk clerk took pity on the bedraggled crew that graced their lobby and offered us some free snacks from the overpriced hotel store.

Minutes later, I lay in bed, listening to light snores from tired girls. Questions plagued me as I fell in and out of sleep: Where do we find courage to do hard things? How do we keep moving when we don't know that things are going to be okay?

The early morning wake-up was painful; my dreams had been peppered with crashes in oversized snow banks and slow-motion spins on black ice. Anxiety and guilt weighed me down as I woke up the girls and hurried them quickly into the van.

The mountain pass was open.

We crept carefully through the canyon that morning. Spots of black ice threatened to de-road us and inattentive truck drivers weaved dangerously through timid traffic, spraying gray slush on my fluid-less windshield. The shadows of dark mountains blocked any natural light that might help me see through the muddy streaks, and I pulled off exits frequently to douse my windows with wiper fluid.

I clenched my jaw and drove.

Four hours later, I breathed a deep sigh, a cocktail of relief and exhaustion, as we pulled into Grand Junction, Colorado. The city bustled around in preparations for Thanksgiving the next day, but the weather was clear. I checked on Denver's blizzard and, as predicted, Colorado had closed the pass again.

We had made it through, barely.

We wound back through southeastern Utah on an uneventful last leg of our trip. We were quiet. Even the girls had felt the wary implications of what would have happened if we had made a misstep. If I had made a misstep.

The weight of responsibility felt heavy as I more cogently thought through our choices of the past 24 hours.

I felt grateful for whatever intrinsic sense of survival and protection we are granted. For the sense of resourcefulness and problem solving that clicks into cognitive place, skills I know aren't built into everyone's framework. I wondered how parents are supposed to stay calm for children when we are struggling to stay calm for ourselves. I wondered how we stayed safe.

How can it be up to me?

I still wonder.

forgiveness.

Can you imagine?

She flew too close to the sun tonight.

My own daring Icarus soared high
with giddiness and power.

She flew upwards with outstretched wings,
gliding on the warm currents of freedom
without watching for her proximity to danger.

And without knowing when to stop flying,
her beautifully crafted wings melted
from her proximity to danger.

And she fell.

She fell from great heights, spiraling in the air as
she raced toward earth, and I feared she'd be
lost forever in the tumultuous, churning sea.

I can't lose her.

I raced to catch her. Melted wings burned me as I
pulled her close, her red face buried into my chest.

She wept from the grief and the guilt
and the grace she needed.

"I'm so sorry, Mom. Can you forgive me?"

Forgiveness.
Can you imagine?

The list of learning and lessons can wait.

She silently begs for a place at the table, a place of warmth that will soothe the wrinkle in her heart. A place where hands will hold her tightly, where she will feel the grace that burns painfully as she accepts it.

She needs compassion, however undeserving she believes she is—a false believe ingrained in the formative minds of our children.

As I hold her close in her discomfort, I whisper in her ear:

You are still so loved.
You are still so good.
You are still so brave.

Forgiveness.
Can you imagine?

Can you imagine catching melted wings from those who flew too far from you?

Could we, in our self-inflicted unworthiness, give and receive the grace that we desperately need?

Could I? Could you?

Will we hold those close who shake with shame, who fight against the intrinsic adversarial voices that whisper rumors of self-loathing?

Will we give place at our table to those whose broken wings require caring for, mercy, and humility?

Forgiveness.
Can you imagine?

not yet

Last night, the snow fell heavily, building tall
barricades onto bare branches and evergreen
boughs. Tree limbs now hang lower than before,
shaking ever so slightly under the weight of
their new burdens; a few sigh in relief as their
spindly arms let the snow slide from their
grasps and drop to the pavement below.

"I'm thirteen. I can do what I want. You
do not have to protect me."

Stubborn teenage refrains echo in the energy
around me as I stare out the window at my world
covered in snow and turmoil, a world where
utter catastrophe reigns while catapulting its
occupants into punctuated grief and loss.

What is protection, after all, my love?

Across our very street, a beautiful, genial soul
mourns the sudden passing of her husband. And our
discourteous, automated world simply moves on,
synchronously ticking from one minute to the next
without regard for her world that has indeed stopped.

I cannot protect you from loss, my girl.

Across the world from our comfortable beds
and curated Instagram feeds, children sleep in
haphazard bunkers while their mothers cradle

the weight of caregiving and their fathers
conscript for an unwarranted national cause.

I cannot protect you from ruthlessness
and tragedy, darling.

Across the shadows of dark networks,
unsuspecting children are silenced, stolen, and
sold to conspiratorial and conniving humans
who should, instead, be saving them.

I cannot protect you from the cruelty and
the effects of others' choices, my love.

But, yes, I absolutely must try to protect you while
also preparing you for this indelible world experience
that will be both unequivocal joy and also the most
untouchable pain. Just a bit longer in my arms before
you cannot be denied your turn to experience it all.

Through the window, a cerulean sky breaks across
the horizon and frames the barricaded branches
against brightness and light; the boughs come
to life and continue to drop their wintry burdens,
carefree and lithesome in the snow's absence.

"I don't want to let go yet," I whisper to the trees. "Not
yet."

A journal entry

7/9/13

Muses of a mother's guilt.

I wish you knew.

I wish you knew how the kisses I place on your cheeks aren't enough to show you just how much you mean to me. The squeezes and snuggles are now exchanged for careless listening and other priorities.

Where did you go?

Where did the time go?

I once snuggled you close to my chest, and now you are so big, so beautiful.

Time is passing without me. Where am I?

I am drifting.

I want to see you. Really see you and pay attention to you and hear you when you call, even if you call wordlessly from the confines of your heart.

I want to listen.

I'm ready to be there.

I miss you.

don't forget

The surprises we find in boxes of miscellany.

A rush of affection filled my chest while pangs
of nostalgia weakened the wall I had built to
move on from the life we used to know.

Our sweet dog died suddenly from cancer
just months after our equally abrupt divorce
and unexpected move from our home.

My incredible oldest babe, who loves so tremendously
large, felt lost in the grief of losing her best friend.
And it consumed much of her very formative years.

Shattered her memories into pieces of heartbreak.

I pulled her close today and whispered tender
thoughts about strength, growth, and deep love.
I showed her this picture. Her voice wavered,
and her beautiful hazels filled with tears.
"Mom," she said. "I am going to keep the tears
in this time. It's time for me to get over it."

I looked fiercely into her pained face.

"Darling. You love so large. Your capacity to feel
for others is your greatest gift, your greatest
strength. Don't get over it. Don't forget. Don't
diminish the depth of love you feel for our past."

And we held each other and wept for the beauty of our difficult past and for the beauty of our bright future, both filled with the deepest of love.

it's okay to be sad

In the back of the Target parking lot, my youngest
daughter wraps her legs around me and buries
her face in my hair. I hold her fiercely against
my chest as I rock her and smooth her hair and
kiss the tears pouring down her cheeks.

She cries for her dad—a heartbreaking
wail of pain and confusion.

I tell her that it's okay to be sad. That it's okay to
cry. That this is hard, the comings and goings
between two homes, two lives, two families.

She watches him walk away and feels the pain
of it all send fresh tears down her face.

And she absolutely must feel it.

She and we and I must learn that for healing—
for grief to loosen its grasp—the requisite is
that we must feel the pain and sorrow and
confusion for as long as it will linger.

That in it we will find resilience
and strength and peace.

We go out to dinner. Giggle with the waitress and
cackle at mom jokes. We top-of-our-lungs sing along
to The Greatest Showman soundtrack while unloading
the dishwasher. We tease and poke and kiss and love.

By the end, she is worn out.

I tuck her tired body into bed as her stuffed animals fill the void next to her chest. I lay beside her on top of her dusty pink ballerina comforter. We give bunny kisses, and she takes deep, heavy breaths, breathing out the last of her residual sobs.

I watch her as she closes her heavy, grief-laden, beautiful eyes.

And she whispers:

"It's okay to be sad."

She squeezed my hand.

Once. Twice. Three times. Four. Five.

She squeezed it five times.

"Dad told me what that means, Mom," she said quietly as I held her. A surge of fresh tears felt hot as they traveled the well-worn paths down my cheeks.

"He did, baby?" I choked over my words as anguish and confusion knotted and entangled deep inside my abdomen.

Just months before, betrayal and lies had broken the marriage I had held so dear. The façade had collapsed, and I was left damaged in its rubble, digging my way out.

"Yeah. He told me each squeeze is a word. I. Love. You. So. Much." She squeezed my hand again and again in sync with each word. She paused. "Did you and Dad do that with each other?"

"Yes, baby, we did," I told her, my voice husky.

I still remember the forested road in rural North Carolina, where it became our thing. A subtle pick-me-up, a secret reminder of how much we loved each other.

We sat in silence. The grief and perplexity enveloped us as we held each other. Words were useless, a blasphemy to the sacred space in which we sat.

So we squeezed hands.

Once.

Twice.

Then three.

And four.

Five times.

I. Love. You. So. Much.

choose me

Choose me, I thought.

Me. Me. Me.

Goosebumps prickle my arms as the cool fall breeze blows through the bleachers. Family members cheering on their softball players are huddled in sweatshirts, beanies and blankets wrapped around shivering bodies as we sit through the last inning of my daughter Kate's blisteringly long U10 softball game.

I stare at my curly-haired kindergartner. At my tall bombshell of a tween. Only twelve feet away from me but in a different world. They shout excitedly at the sight of a woman they know. A woman they love. A woman who loves them.

It's not me.

My girls rush to her side. They call her name. They jump on her. Touch her face. Crave her presence and attention.

I am here, too, I think. *Right here. Always here.*

I am here, yes, but on the other side of an invisible divide.

I am here. She is there.

And, tonight, they choose her.

Old wounds open as embedded emotional
shrapnel twists inside my heart, piercing me deeper.
Leftover from battles with pain and change, I have
tried to heal with sharp fragments still inside.

My youngest laughs and runs on the concrete,
slipping on the loose red sand that has migrated from
home plate. She cries. And although I am less than five
feet away, my girl reaches for another to comfort her.

This woman scoops Scarlett up into an embrace.

I let her.

Lily, my oldest, snuggles with her and laughs
with her. Shows her silly emoji texts on her
phone. Catches my eye and smiles briefly.

I feel grief, but I cannot feel sadness. My eyes fill
but do not weep. My chest, heavy to the point of
breaking, expands with air; I hold my breath to
gain control. I let it blow slowly through my lips.

Scarlett wraps her legs around the woman's
waist, her curls falling gently as she nestles
into the curve of this woman's body. I watch
lips that aren't mine kiss the top of Scarlett's
head and rock her, soothe her, placate her.

A familiar man bearing nachos and cotton candy
approaches the woman holding Scarlett. He sits next
to them. Wraps his arms around her and my girls.
Makes Scarlett laugh and wipes tears out of her eyes.

For 12 years, I loved him, and now
I watch him love another.

She is his.

They hold Scarlett. They hold my baby, the one I birthed and nursed and nourish and cherish. My baby, who isn't a baby anymore but is long legs and toothless smiles, with whom I sit at night as she fears the dark. With whom I sing and read and fall asleep on couches and ballerina bed covers.

Mine.

But is also theirs.

I feel discomfort. I feel peace. I feel empty, but I feel the wholeness of emptiness. It's a kind of peace set in the jagged, sharp edges of the realization that **the purpose of pain is to enlarge the capacities of our love.**

There is purpose in pain. Love is the purpose.

The largest kind of love requires courage found in the hidden corners of our hearts, intermixed with the heartache that we have been afraid of and may be unwilling to touch. In order to feel our deepest capacity for love, we have to be willing to sit in the discomfort and burden of our grief.

And that's a damn tall order.

Because we are never fully healed, there's no summit to conquer. No titles to win or medals to collect. Growth through grief isn't a sprint. It's endurance training.

And sometimes, the pain feels too great,
and the hurt is unendurable.

But if, just IF, we can take steps to undertake what
feels like an impossible task—this love will change us.
This love will give rich meaning to our brokenness.
This love will forge deep intrinsic strength.

We cannot, however, underestimate our timing:
We must be handled carefully as we sit with the
parts of us that are too hot to touch. Too soon,
and we can disrupt the healing patterns we are
trying to pursue. But when we are malleable
enough to be molded and shaped, real bravery
is sitting in the discomfort of this change.

Remember, love can be larger than
we ever suspected it could be.

Lily notices me sitting alone, wanders to
my side, and huddles with me under my
warm blanket. She kisses my forehead.

"Mom. You okay? You seem sad." She leans against
me. It fills my chest with courage. "I love you, momma."

She walks back to sit with her sisters, her dad,
her other mom, all of whom love her so dearly.

I watch her go.

A pang of loss swells inside my chest. I
let it sit there, stirring inside me.

And I turn to watch the softball game.

tragic beauty

Parenthood is tragically beautiful.

In truth, I face constantly the absolute denial that it's not exactly what I had expected. It's not pretty pink bows, little harmonious ditties of happy families. Sometimes I get angry—the script I had written for what I thought should be just... isn't.

I hadn't prepared for this.

The only way I can possibly write about this now is because my girls are giggling downstairs, laughing about little crushes and YouTube snippets as they chase each other in socks on the wood floor. Parenthood is much easier to digest when the tension is deflected for a moment, when difficulty is shoved aside for the infrequent moments of peace. There are real moments of gentleness and calm.

Sometimes I forget that.

Because really, no one can prepare us for the humility of hurt, the animosity and anger that burns in hearts and heads. The utter exasperation from stubborn defiance that helps shape these burgeoning adults (or possible criminals, who knows).

No one tells us that we have to learn how to love specifically AND differently from how we might know how to love. That loving requires growth on our parts as parents as much as on their part as kids.

Parenthood is building walls to protect and breaking them down just as quickly.

No one tells us what to do when a headstrong daughter doesn't want to show up to Thanksgiving dinner under any circumstances. Who knows what to do when cruel and vicious insults poison the air? What should we do when blame turns us into monsters—when it's our damn fault for doing what we thought was best?

Being a safe place is dangerous mental territory. What do we do on the days when it's all too much to hold? Days when we feel absolutely broken?

I don't have an answer.

Usually, I feel defeated for a while. I go to sleep. Sit outside on the porch. Go for a walk. Lift heavy weights. Cry. Hope things will be better tomorrow. Apologize. And then repeat the cycle tomorrow.

Being broken can feel lonely, but we are never alone.

There's a world of perfectly imperfect parents out there, weighed down by our inadequacies and buoyed by the empathy shared by the likes of them.

Let's find each other.

part 4:
jesus loves the sinners except for me

"Faith is to be awake
And to be awake is for us to think
And for us to think is to be alive."
-twenty one pilots

background

The Church of Jesus Christ of Latter-day Saints is often referred to as the LDS church; members of its congregations are called LDS or, more colloquially, "the Mormons." Founded by Joseph Smith in 1844, the LDS Church follows many tenets of mainstream Christianity but, among other things, believes in latter-day prophets, a more specific plan of salvation, and another book of scripture called the Book of Mormon.

Mormons (as a whole) are well-known for their abstinence from premarital sex and what are considered "harmful substances," namely hot drinks (coffee and tea), alcohol, and illicit drugs. Globally, the Mormon church sends out over 53,000 missionaries a year and contributes to massive humanitarian aid outreach programs. The hierarchy of the LDS church is substantially male, and bishops are male ecclesiastical leaders responsible for the welfare of their Mormon congregations.

Members of the LDS faith are often called to clarify sticky portions of their church history, especially in regards to polygamy, which was practiced by members of the LDS church and its leaders in mainstream Mormonism for over half a century. This practice was outlawed in 1890 and fell out of use; however, fundamentalist denominations of the Mormon religion still actively practice this doctrine.

washed clean

Membership in The Church of Jesus Christ of Latter-day Saints begins with baptism.

My parents, both converts to the LDS faith, reared me in its tenets from birth. My mom joined the church at fifteen after good friends brought her around to church activities. It was a heart-based choice—the church felt like home back then, and she has beseechingly clung to it ever since. She remains the only member of the LDS faith in her family. My mustache-donning dad, however, was firmly anti-religion as a young adult and identified the church as an object to disprove. He later joined the same faith he had sought to discredit.

Growing up within a strict, conservative culture was, simply, a part of my childhood. I learned both secular and spiritual precepts at the hands of rule-following parents and under the guidance of a well-organized, task-oriented religion.

They believed.

I was taught to believe at all costs.

When I was eight years old, I chose to be baptized.

The tender age of eight is not randomized but is instead the age at which we are taught our personal accountability begins. At this age, we are washed clean from our childhood sins and are blessed with special gifts from the Holy Spirit to guide us through our lives. This ritual act of baptism by immersion is the first step on the pathway—and the only way—to real salvation.

Children in the LDS church prepare readily for this day. They learn parables, mark scripture, and sing pretty ditties in harmonies about following the examples of Jesus Christ. Members of the church preach sermons on the blessings of baptism into the one true church.

My dad stood next to me in the church baptismal font and baptized me by immersion—an important connotation. Other churches, I was taught, may have baptized their members, but we, members of the one true gospel, were baptized by immersion like our Savior, Jesus Christ. We follow His example, and on the day of my baptism, by-standing male witnesses verified that, indeed, no portion of my white, borrowed baptismal gown floated to the surface of the water as I plugged my nose and held my breath to be washed clean of childhood sins.

It's fascinating what we remember from the formative years of our childhood.

I still remember the mildly chlorinated smell of the small changing room adjacent to the font, the room in which I hid years later as I skipped weekly Sunday School classes.

I remember the long braid woven into my wet hair as I dressed quickly from baptismal frock to a conservative Sunday dress, pulling tights uncomfortably onto damp legs as I tried to hurry: Everyone was waiting for me.

It was a celebration of my faith, which ended with a benediction and box-mixed brownies on small, wrinkled napkins.

I was clean, my sins washed away.

Until I wasn't.

disappointing god

My sister sat nervously in the office of her bishop. She was turning eight, which meant it was time for her to choose to be baptized. Before her baptism, she was required to meet with the bishop to answer questions about her faith.

These questions, common to more experienced members of the church, include: *Do you believe that God is our Eternal Father? Do you believe that Jesus Christ is the Son of God, the Savior and Redeemer of the world? Do you believe the Church and gospel of Jesus Christ have been restored through the Prophet Joseph Smith?*

"What happens if I don't want to be baptized?" my sister had asked the bishop.

"Well, technically you don't have to," said her bishop, looking uncomfortable. "But your parents would be very disappointed and so would Heavenly Father."

This mentality of needing to earn God's love permeated my sister's and my faith-developing years. His love became a love to earn and to claim based on a checklist of prayers said, scriptures read, and repentance from sins. For many years, we exhausted ourselves in the pursuit of perfection's suffocating regime.

God is love, but I just wanted God to love me.

falling out of truth

Falling out of truth
breaks the hearts
and stains the cheeks of those
who taught me
who raised me
who prayed for me
who broke bread with me.

They grieve for me,
as I fall from the grace they have preached to me,
and I become a statistic –
the one alone
from the ninety and nine,
one they have lost
one they must bring back to the fold of those
who exhaust themselves
in service to their truths.

Because I,
a brilliant magnanimous mind,
was tamed
subdued
molded
by thoughts that conflicted,
by beliefs that I didn't understand.

But still, God, falling out of truth
conflicts me
tricks me
bewitches me

as promised blessings disappear
behind veils of judgement
and disappointment
and subtle reminders to others
to not be influenced by my betrayal.

I can't unremember weekly lessons
of strict parochial teachings
or blanket judgments
or the rules
that would keep me safe
but to keep me safe
from what,
I wonder?

I am confused.
Is the God who loved me then
the same
who cannot love me now?

And, oh, I love my God
but I can't seem to lift my heart to ask Him –
Can I pray to you as I fall out of truth?
I feel too lowly
too broken
too far away
from the grace that was once mine.

Can I still talk to you, God?
Because I'm the same as I once was,
when I was shrouded in faith.
My heart beats the same number of beats
and my eyes see the same beauty.
My compassion to give is great
as is the love I carry in me.

Am I worthy to you, God?
because I'm not to
the preachers and the teachers
and the family of mine
who sit in the hopes that I'll return
and serve the God
who loves them,
so one day we can rejoice
in a happy heaven
and sing the old Hallelujah.

And here I wonder
to those who plead
for my happiness
for my return
for my oaths
and forever faith –

Did the Christ who gave Himself to you
give himself for me, too?
If He still paid for me with His sufferings,
why do you take my sins on you too
with pained eyes
and strained hearts
and love conditional?

Is His grace sufficient only
for what
you
believe?

At times falling out of truth
feels more tragic
than
falling out of love.

And so I beg you, God –
keep me broken,
keep me wild,
God
as I fall out of truth.

jesus can still love me

She and I chatted briefly at the gas station entrance as we did whenever our caffeine runs coincided. This time, though, her eyes darted back to my face after glancing at my bare thighs.

This behavior has become quite the norm.

As I transitioned out of the LDS church, my wardrobe choices changed; I now find clothes that compliment my body shape and are more revealing than what I had previously worn while actively involved in my religion. While this sounds like I'm walking around with my breasts hanging out, all it means is that my shorts have a shorter inseam, and many of my shirts no longer have sleeves. Everything is still tucked nicely and neatly in their bra cups, Mom.

However, in my many years as a member of this religion, church policy and culture expected (demanded?) knee-length shorts and sleeves on shirts, so baring my thighs in public could seem a questionable choice to others who belong to the same religion. Bare shoulders are an indicator that, no, I'm not wearing the modest, religion-based undergarments predominantly utilized by active members of the LDS church. These knee-length, cap-sleeve garments fit under a member's clothing and are worn as a sign of worthiness.

I'm now considered unworthy for
choosing to bare parts of my body that
were previously very, very covered.

I grew up with modesty as my baseline. I was
taught that modesty matters, that "modest is
hottest." High necklines and covered shoulders
seemed to be the only thing available in
the shops on the pathway to salvation.

In the guidelines for the youth of the LDS church,
modesty in dress is a huge component:

> "Never lower your standards of dress. Do
> not use a special occasion as an excuse to
> be immodest. When you dress immodestly,
> you send a message that is contrary to your
> identity as a son or daughter of God. You
> also send the message that you are using
> your body to get attention and approval.
>
> Immodest clothing is any clothing that is
> tight, sheer, or revealing in any other manner.
> Young women should avoid short shorts
> and short skirts, shirts that do not cover the
> stomach, and clothing that does not cover the
> shoulders or is low-cut in the front or the back.
>
> Show respect for the Lord and yourself
> by dressing appropriately.
>
> Ask yourself, 'Would I feel comfortable with my
> appearance if I were in the Lord's presence?'"

As preached by the LDS church, modesty is integral
to our relationship with our Heavenly Father.

It's a sense of humility, of unpretentiousness. A reserved measure of self—we should behave in a teachable, submissive, delicate, and simple way.

To be frank, I do believe the pursuit of modesty is more damaging and egocentric than it is helpful.

As a teenager, trying to wear anything inappropriate around my eagle-eyed mother was exhausting. Eventually, I gave up sneaking around, rolling up the hems of long shorts, or wearing illicit tank tops just because she was so damn consistent in her rule expectations.[4] Essentially, if my clothing was mother-approved, it was appropriate enough for a nun convention, let alone a church function.

On one particular Sunday, my mom walked up to me at church, eyed my knee-length khaki pencil skirt, and frantically patted me down like a TSA officer hyped on an energy drink. The skirt had a small slit in the front—if you were lucky, you could see the fullness of my kneecaps when I walked (and as I'm sure you're aware, knobby teenage knees are super attractive).

"What are you doing, Mom?" I asked.

"Brother [insert generic man's name] told me you had your skirt on backward. I was just checking," she said.

This behavior from members of our congregation was not new. Church leaders often commented on my dress; one even marked on my legs in a black Sharpie the length my shorts were supposed to be.

---

[4]   As an adult, I'm actually very grateful for her damn consistency. I am now a damn consistent parent.

"Brother [insert another generic man's name here] came to me and said your shirt was too revealing."

"Sister [you get the point] told me about your inappropriate shorts at camp."

"The way you dress is a temptation for my son."

Why, pray tell, is my salvation based on whether or not my shoulders are covered? Listen, I try to be a good human. I pay my taxes and give to charity and volunteer and hold doors open and put my shopping carts back.

To answer the above question: Would I feel comfortable with my appearance if I was standing in front of the Lord?

The answer is undeniably, yes. I would. Bare thighs and all.

Jesus loves the sinners.

He can still love me, even if He can see my shoulders.

god-shaped holes

the truth of the matter
is that there is no truth
that is one-size-fits-all

a master manipulator,
truth is an adjustable hatband
that shrinks and swells
to fit the shape of
you
me
he and she,
now and what was.

truths fit conveniently
into god-shaped holes
where we
generalize beliefs,
label at our peril,
and monopolize pieces and parts
of religion
so we have soft places to land.

truths cannot be Truths
when we
think
live
breathe
differently—
when your bibles and mine
disagree.

to those who preach
concrete truth?
by all means,
mix your cement
and build your mansions
in heaven

but don't expect me
to help mortar your walls,
trapping my questions
in a box
to set upon a shelf of faith
for the eternities.

land softly where you want.

i will do the same.

sad heaven

A strong, overarching tenet of the LDS church is that families can be together forever, even into the eternities. This idea comforts the hearts of many, especially when families experience the death of a loved one. With the concept of eternal families so embedded in the Mormon dogma, death loses its sting as the eternities will reunite families in a grand celebration.

I was taught that we would always see each other again—that death is not the end. The sacrifices we made on earth as members of the one true church would exalt us above the rest. Once we are removed from "this mortal coil" (coined by Shakespeare, used by my dad), we will live together as an eternal family in the highest hierarchy of a happy heaven.

[Insert record scratch here.]

Let's amend that statement.

We can live in a happy heaven **only if** all the family members have stayed active in the LDS faith, have kept all of God's commandments, and still attend the sacred temple, which teaches its attendees the promises necessary to enter the kingdom of God with their families.

This future eternal happiness is tricky when someone leaves the religious flock and looks elsewhere to seek joy and authenticity.

The alternative is sad heaven.

I remember when I sat down with my family and explained that I was taking a step back from my church attendance. My inactivity in the LDS church was not out of convenience, no, but was instead an intentional decision made as I examined the values of my own life and whether they aligned with the principles of the LDS church.

As many of my family members are strong, active members of the LDS faith, this was a shock, especially since I had been a very strong member of the church for 35 years. I volunteered constantly, worshipped reverently, attended the sacred temple, and kept the promises I made to God within those walls.

Families can be together forever, except for me, the great apostate.

Someone once told me, "Just stop going to church—it's not that big of a deal."

It's not that simple. It's not like switching pharmacies or changing dentists. I was raised to believe I belonged to the one true gospel of Jesus Christ, and everything we did as members of that church was in order to return to Him again in righteousness and glory.

By leaving, I've cut down my branch of the family tree with a proverbial hatchet. In the eyes of my family and their faith, my decision to step away affects even the eternal future of my posterity.

Losing my faith has separated us, my family and me. It's a chasm that broke apart the faithful from the faithless. I remember my mom crying as she said, "I'm just so sad thinking that we won't be together forever."

This happy heaven of theirs is tinged with grief. The bright heaven they once imagined grows dimmer as family members retreat into the darkened shadows of unbelief.

I sit now, feeling the grief of having left. The juxtaposition is real—the tenets of the LDS church brought me peace and comfort at times of my life when my spirit was threatened, when my divorce tossed me into despair, and when I questioned my purpose and identity.

I've felt as much love as I have felt confusion for this religion that I belonged to. I don't follow its principles, and I don't ascribe to its beliefs. Yet, I can't disremember the goodness and identity I felt within its walls—the same goodness that doesn't complete me anymore.

I grieve that I can no longer be a part of the happy heaven my family believes in, although they still belong in mine.

It's tricky, this sad heaven I've chosen.

part 5:
the complexity of self-compassion

"Do not assume that he who seeks
to comfort you now,
lives untroubled among the simple and quiet
words that sometimes do you good...
Were it otherwise, he would never have
been able to find these words."

— Rainer Maria Rilke

my mind is a junk drawer

The junk drawer crashed to the floor, spilling its contents over the square footage of my entire kitchen.

Out of what I can only assume was spite and maliciously poor timing, the silver knob of the junk drawer had caught snugly in the pocket of the jacket tied around my waist. I whipped around, felt the pull of the drawer on its tracks, the tug of my jacket behind me, and I quickly calculated the risk of acute back injury if I tried to gymnastic my way into saving the drawer from its impending fall.

My lumbar region silently thanked me as I stared at the pile of, well, junk, that had amassed on the floor.

My mind, a little numb after a difficult morning raising volatile tweens and a senile six-year-old, spun mercilessly like the Big Wheel on The Price is Right. I was a final contestant at the Showcase Showdown of emotions, and the 20-sided Big Wheel was boop-boop-booping dangerously close to "ugly-crying" and "rage-arson" (I believe it landed on "foggy and numb, go get a Coke Zero and a cookie from Crumbl").

I sat cross-legged on my dirty floor, watching out for errant nails and thumbtacks that could prove risky to my derriere. Tape, old batteries, probably about 37 lip balms (I have a problem, just shut up about it), capless markers, a now-cracked thermometer, a stick of tropical-smelling deodorant, and every Allen wrench I'd ever used to assemble some swear-worthy piece of IKEA furniture obstructed my vision, my expectation of normalcy.

All my junk was visible.

Have you ever really thought about the contents of your junk drawer? For months (yeah, okay, years), my useful and useless had shared the same dark space, had been relegated to a place without definition, tangled in each other's wires and cords, stuck to the backs of wrinkled post-it notes.

The useful and useless now lay
scattered visibly in the open.

I sorted through the items, separating them into what to keep and what to send to the recycle bin (and the landfill, you are so welcome, Mother Earth).

I re-homed the junk drawer and filled it with items like long lighters for candles (and arson, if the opportunity presents itself), my collection of small tools, and a few pens.

Homeless remnants litter the floor. I swept up the broken objects, tetanus-loving nails, old bobby pins, a felt Santa?, and sticky hands that had lost the sticky into a dustpan, then emptied its contents into the garbage.

Clean.

Free from the useless, from the garbage cluttering my spaces, from the burden of dead weight.

And it's not lost on me:

My mind is a junk drawer, weighed down by homeless, leftover thoughts that need a place to stay.

Useless, dominant thoughts whisper,

"You're not enough, Kiera."

"You don't belong here."

"You have to be perfect to be loved, didn't you know that?"

Negative energy, fears, perfectionism, rejection, and inadequacy clutter the space inside me, and what hurts the most is that

At one point or another, I let them all in.

I let these useless thoughts flirt and manipulate, let them wrap themselves around the power that exists within me, let them abuse the neuroplasticity that gives me strength and teaches me to grow.

In my ignorance, I hadn't noticed just how quickly I had become so overrun with nonessentials and burdened by figuratively broken and bent objects, with anxiety that plastered itself as propaganda on the walls of my cerebrum.

So much useless has taken up so much space.

And so, I'm sweeping it all up. The outcome is not immediate, of course. Sweeping up the trash takes time and practice. Clearing the cobwebs of resiliency and self-compassion requires ME to give the task habitual and active participation.

But I will do it anyway.

The space in my mind is going for much higher rent than it used to be.

in recovery

Hello, my name is Kiera, and I am an addict.

That's right, an addict.

And although you'll come to find that while I dip my toes in many pools of addictive behavior, my truly challenging vice doesn't come from food, exercise, hobbies or diet soda.

I am a perfectionist.

A diluted perfectionist these days. Perhaps even in recovery, one might say.

I feel a certain freedom now, a sort of laissez-faire mentality that has burst from my hyper-focused brain and helped me recalibrate, helped me find solid footing among the crags and footholds of a hyper-consuming condition.

A real mental condition.

This fragmented way of thinking caught hold of me when I was very young, as I mistakenly thought that being loved required a certain amount of perfection. To be seen as an equal or be treated with respect and loyalty or, I admit, admiration, demanded a certain unyielding commitment to success and excellence.

A seed of desire for this deluded way of thinking germinated inside my mind, and I cultivated it with nourishment and encouragement. For a brief season,

I thought I could make it work. I thought that I could be the one to do it all. To do everything and anything.

It would be me.

And it was here in this cold, unreachable place that I abandoned necessary self-compassion, where I left divine grace and intrinsic worthiness laying out by the recycle bin.

Everything that mattered lay rejected and ignored, waiting for the garbage truck to haul it away.

Until the day came that I lay rejected, thrown out like rubbish, my company only scraps of leftover food and empty Amazon boxes.

I was trashed.

Yet, it was there in my despair that I found the grace I had once abandoned so easily, and it was there in the gutters of rejection that I remembered my worth. I found my self-compassion, foggy and muddy from being left out in the storms, requiring some elbow grease for rehabilitation.

But I found myself again.

I am still an addict.

Yet, I'm warmer now. A milder, more temperate version of the Kiera who had given herself away to impossibilities.

However, as we addicts know, cognitive demand is desperately unforgiving, and I often feel the lure of perfectionism lurking inside me, waiting for my walls to fall so I'll forget myself again.

So, here I tell you:

I will always be recovering.

I can do anything but not everything.

And that's okay.

I worry.

Unavoidably so.

Tendrils of anxiety twist and bend and
curl and spiral into tightly wound springs,
catastrophe cocked and loaded.

Worries as rough and ripped as hangnails
that snag on fabrics of thought.

Voices warn me to let go of the uncontrollable,
to stop selling my proverbial birthright for
the valueless messes of pottage that burden
my mind. But I, like Esau, choose poorly.

And I worry.

I worry about my growing babies.

About whether or not I can give them all they
need for their foggy futures. All the tools and
tricks of the trade. The emotional resilience
required to navigate impossible decisions.

I worry about time.

I glorify the busy but drown in mindless scrolling.
I rush. I waffle. I lay in silence and stare at the
ceiling. I wish for more time to make up for the
lost time. And time, that tricky thief, mocks
my inconsistency by keeping what is hers and
giving me the same as everyone else.

I worry about cost.

Is it quality over quantity or quantity over quality? My bank account dictates this answer as I mechanically buy bulk, haggle over cents per ounce, place generic pasta inside my cart, and search my browser for mediocre coupons. How far will I drive to save 14 cents on a gallon of gas?

I worry.

I worry about not being enough. About letting my intrinsic potential escape like sand through open fingers of inadequacy and laziness.

I worry.

About making mistakes that can't be fixed and trapping myself inside self-constructed boxes of has-beens and who-cares.

I worry about finding love and losing love and forgetting the cost of falling in and out of love.

And so I worry.

But sometimes, if only briefly, the wild gale of worry settles as the eye of the hurricane passes over me.

And I feel contentment.

And when that happens, I pack the sunshine and wonder into my pocket and hold it close to my heart. For strength. For resilience. For the future.

But otherwise —

I'll worry.

just passing through

I feel a mess inside,
twisted and scarred,
burned to hot ash
and left to regrow.

Gnarled roots
and thick branches
hedge my way
as I bleed
and limp
and cry out

but who else will cut through the tangle inside?

Barbed thistles and
cunning vines
catch me and
claw me and
mock me.

I feel choked by
necessities
and burdened by
impossibilities
and trapped
by duty
by fear
by expectation

and I will stay trapped
here

inside
my own mind

inside the scuttle
until I can carve my way
through the briars
and the shadows
and break free.

Then

the tangles
and brambles
and thorns
will bow to me

as I say,
"Just passing through,"
my confidence
and self-compassion
at the helm
of my prowess.

I am a large.

I think large.

I feel large.

My stature. My personality. The volume of my voice. The height of my heels. I wear larges, from my shirts to my size 10 shoes.

I am a large.

The healthy numbers on the scale, the size of muscles I want. The weight I can lift.

My family. My voice. My laugh. The way I love. The depth of loyalty I feel. The plans for my future. The potential I feel for myself that sits so intimately inside me.

Who I AM and who I can be. *How* I can be.

Whom I can help. Whom I can love and who will let me love them. The talents I possess and the type of mother I want to be. The dining room table that holds chairs full of family and friends.

The hurt and grief and the voids that sit untouched inside my heart. The size of my Coke Zero fountain drink. The unwritten dreams I have for my girls' potentials and desires. My extensive knowledge of swear words. My minivan mileage from wanderlusty cross-country tours.

The pride and courage that fill me, but also the failure and discouragement that plague me. The power and tenacity and drive to see how high I can climb, but also the knowledge of how far I can and will fall.

The walls I build.

How loud I listen to my workout music. The motivation I have to succeed. To push. To pull. To hope for my future. The contagious smile I get when I laugh. The connections with those I love. The high highs and the low lows, the addictions, the to-do lists littering my fridge door.

The fire I feel for passion and beauty and ideas.

I live and love large.

Others have tried to shrink my size. I'm too loud. Too embarrassing. Too overwhelming. Too many, too much, too big.

But I'll never make myself small again. Never let the influences of those whose words burn with hate and jealousy and ridicule try to shrink my influence. I won't make myself smaller than I am.

I feel large.

I think large.

I am a large.

the women who stand in front of mirrors

we are vultures of our own destruction, picking
apart the meat from our bones as we reduce and
scavenge our bodies into carcasses of self-loathing.

what else are we to do?

we've auctioned off pieces of ourselves to the
lowest bidder since Mother Eve's enlightenment;

why, isn't the devil in Eden's Garden the very first
influencer?

stupid things people have said to me

"With all those scars, you'll never be a leg model."

My boss at a high school job: "I hate it
when fat girls have pretty faces."

Him, grabbing onto my bra fat: "What is this?"

pride

My smile.

A broad, smirky grin that kisses high
cheekbones and tugs at deep dimples.

Irreplaceable. Untouched by the mimicry of superficiality.

My smiles aren't rare in delivery, but seldom do I share
the ones that are
unhindered
uncontaminated
unbroken
& proud.

I smile like this

at remembering.
at growth.
at fear's feeble attempts.
at the heartache that gave way
for this smile's beginning.

Full circle. All-encompassing.
Rare as finite jewels.
Infinitely more precious.

the procession

The cluster of cars around me was stuck in
traffic on an inbound freeway exit lane, inching
ahead as the overhead traffic lights taunted
us by flashing their greens our way.

I tapped impatiently on the steering wheel as I
chronically checked my clock and fixed out-of-place
strands of hair. Spotify songs seemed to play at cut
time, racing unnecessarily through their love lyrics and
fight anthems as I crept along the lanes of the exit.

Anxious rage bubbled at my unpunctuality, at the
thought of missing my flight, at the mere stupidity of
traffic during early afternoon in downtown Salt Lake.

"This is such a waste of my time," I thought angrily.

I noticed the triple windows first. The shiny black
limo, dated but clean, flanked my left side, and I
stared curiously at its tinted windows, at its somber
driver, at the mortuary name inscribed on its doors.

A funeral procession.

The black sedan at its head carried white flags as it
ushered the great hearse along the route to burial.

The procession moved ahead, and through
the glass, images of the bereaved smeared
my vision and imprinted on my memory—an

older woman, weeping. A bald man, comforting children. Vacant eyes stared ahead blankly.

I sat quietly now.

The reality of watching grief snake its way along my side unsettled me. I invaded their privacy with my selfish, penetrating gaze.

One set of eyes caught mine as I stared— her eyes glued to me for many moments as her vehicle moved past.

"I'm sorry," I whispered as the procession moved out of sight, each car clinging to the others' bumpers, shoring up the mutual strength to murmur final goodbyes.

My drive finished uneventfully, though the marquee of the mourning scrolled through my consciousness.

The thing about grief, you see, is the respect and beauty it demands.

Grief radiates the need for honor—for us to honor the space, the loss, the memory. It's neither a burden nor a release, but maintains the need to be nurtured, cradled in the arms of those who can respect its medley of loss and self-discovery.

We will grow through grief while not outgrowing grief.

That's the journey.

champion

"Lean on me
when you're not strong,"
I whisper to myself
as I walk through the swarm
of my own critical voices,
clamoring with chaos
and singing hymns of falsities.

I step inside the ring
to fight the fear itself,
with fists I often use
to bruise my own heart
and beat down my shoulders,
the same shoulders that should poise
with confidence
with pride
with identity.

This challenger
knows my footwork,
my thoughts,
my vulnerabilities,
because

she is me.

I flinch with each blow,
with each traitorous jab
and every Judas left hook.
I'm up against the ropes.
I fall.

Until I hear my own voice
pounding in my ears,
fueled by adrenaline
and self-advocacy:

"Get up.
Show up for yourself."

I stand once again.
I break the patterns.
I don't run from myself.

Champion.

am I

The warm June breeze tangles my hair and breathes
life into a muggy afternoon.
Jeweled dragonflies and schools of minnows
flirt with the surface of the river.
And I wonder
if they see each other
if the dragonfly wants to dip beneath the water
if the minnow longs for wings.

The silver-haired Black man loops around the inlet for
the third time.
Tall, with a genial face.
Could've played basketball.
His long, tired legs thud on the ground as he runs
heavy and
dragging.
But he runs.

A broken-down car sits in the same corner of the
parking lot as it did two days ago,
rear tires weighed down
by the worldly possessions of its homeless inhabitants.
What did they bring with them?
A bald man in cutoff jeans opens the passenger door,
gingerly takes off his shoes
before he sits inside
his home.

An ice cream truck chimes a faint melody at the nearby
ball fields.

I can almost taste the tingle of a root beer popsicle.
It used to be two quarters
or five dimes
or 49 pennies and a Canadian nickel.
I'd still buy one.

Behind me, an old fisherman checks his three lines in the water.
He belts Aretha, interrupting the sounds of rustling leaves and ball game cheers.
Baritone,
wavering,
husky.
I could listen to him all afternoon.

The wind, still steady and whistling, pushes the current against the grassy shore.
It laps against the stones
by my black Converse shoes,
monotonous,
consistent.
And I ask:

Does the water ever want to push back
against the wind?
Stubbornly,
defiantly,
choosing its own way.

Or does it glide seamlessly where the wind takes it,
for experience,
for change,
open to the new?
Trusting in the wind as it explores
every crag and cove.

And the wind that breathes life into sails and shares
dandelion wishes–
an invisible force, with intrinsic power to create
new life
new energy
new change.
The same wind transforms from slight into storms,
turns breezes into beasts,
twists wisps into whirlwinds,
wild with passionate fury.

And I think,
am I the patience of the old man checking his lines,
am I the persistence of the runner,
am I the willingness of the water,

or

am I the wind?

Sit with me?

I've been holding tightly to an uncomfortable truth.

I have cringed deeply at this part of my story, fought the necessity of admittance, felt the white-hot embarrassment of misunderstanding. Tendrils of fear-based insecurity mock me: "Isolate this. Ignore it. Keep it intensely private and feel its weighty burden." And so I tucked this part of me away in the quiet, dangerous shadows where we hide our shortcomings.

Until tonight.

———————————

Look at me, please.

I can't hear you. Not all the way.

Look at me, please, while I watch your lips craft the letters and words and sounds that develop into pleasant conversations and stories–the ones that nurture delicate laughs and deep connections.

Look at me, please, so I can be a part of the stories that you share.

What you say and what I hear is a complex puzzle. Soundalike digraphs and vowel blends and consonants float in disassociated patterns as my brain Sherlocks a thousand options into creating cogent answers that fit the context of our discussion.

I can't hear the sweet nothings you whisper into my ear or the hushed undertones tucked in at bedtime. I can't hear playground secrets or feel the simplicity of understanding quiet speech.

But

I can see the bright lights in your eyes. I see your lips curl into smiles and stories. I see the dimples and lines on your cheeks. I see your mouth twist into shapes of laughter, of worry, of contentedness. I listen to your words by seeing the raw beauty and grief and peace and hope carved into your face.

I can't hear you. Not all the way.

But I can see you.

Look at me, please.

getting dressed

I slip a worn, gray t-shirt over my black Calvin Klein bra
and settle into comfortable restlessness
under a rose-colored sweatshirt.
I wire a smile that masks the anxiety
I snuck into my pockets.

I layer skinny jeans with stubbornness and pluck
while my inner monologue condescends the belly fat
around my middle,
all because my black joggers need a wash and so does
my mouth —
my mom says I swear too much, and it's not attractive.

I smooth lotion into the deep lines of tension I wear
across my forehead
but leave the crinkles from uninhibited laughter in the
crow's feet around my eyes.
I don't wear much makeup on the weekends; already,
unknown fears contour the shadows of my
cheekbones and highlight my mistakes.

Dry shampoo lifts my hair for one more day,
and I run my fingers through my healing self-concept
to shake out
the tangles.
Vitamin D and blue skies and smiles from
my teenager lift me like helium.

I use nimble fingers to tie the laces of my Chucks
and then to tie distressing thoughts–one to the next,
a bed sheet train inside my brain of obtrusive assumptions
without regard for propriety.

I wrap myself in warmth and worry
and head out into the cold, laden with gloves and scarves
and the consistent burden
of not being enough.

i heard her knocking

i heard her knocking—
pounding incessantly
on the door and
calling me by name.

no.
i won't let her in.

she leaves with a grin,
confident and
malevolent.

flighty and swift,
she visits each of us —
we hear her calling out
to open our doors.

no.
don't let her in
to saturate your soul
with loathing
and wound your wonder
with her poison.

she says she's me
and you
and all the women who stare into mirrors,

but she's an imposter,
a shadow,
a fraud

whispering doubts.

no.
i won't let her in.

the woman in the shadows

Someone is following me, lurking in slate shadows, hidden in every cobwebbed corner.

She's a familiar presence, a sort of intimate figment whose hazel eyes burn into mine as I unexpectedly catch her glance.

Those eyes. I've seen them before.

Crow's feet crinkle the corners of her eyes, accompanying the crease of a dimpled smile, and I hear contagious, carbonated laughter.

Her warm eyes encourage me to find the bravery within, and I do as I step into pools of the unknown.

She's everywhere, reminding me to look up. To take my place. To stand tall with confident posture. To inhale deep breaths of the unexpected.

I feel safe in her trustworthy presence as she reminds me to ignore criticism from those who don't matter.

And one day I realize: This woman in the shadows

is me.

you already are

What if you don't have to earn it?

What if you intrinsically *are*?

We are bred for fierce competition, for measures of success and ladder-climbing. Our statuses are based on the whens of becoming, achieving, and belonging.

But, wait.

Why must we earn the right to be?

Do you have to win a race before you become a runner? Or, are you a runner simply when you run? Am I a teacher only because my pay stub says I am? Do I need to wait until my book is published before I can claim the right to "author"?

Does your daughter earn the right to be an engineer only after years of higher education, or is she one simply because she chooses to use creativity and imagination to construct, failure after failure? What about those artists who've never sold a painting but speak the language of colors and brush strokes?

Our tendency to wait before claiming a title–is that based in "because someone said so," or society's expectation of "you are not until you earn the right to be"? Is it because we could "do so much more" before we feel confident accepting and nurturing our own labels?

I disagree with all of it.

I disagree because everything that you want to be exists inside of you. Now, don't misunderstand. I'm a believer in hard work and tenacity and determination. But make no mistake, you are not responsible for pleasing society's view of **what is** before you lay claim to what you want to be.

I once needed a gentle reminder of this myself from someone whose words sit deeply inside my chest.

Let me be your reminder.

You. Already. Are.

part 6:
who will stop me?

"Do you mean to tell me that you're thinking seriously of building *that way*, when and if you are an architect?"
"Yes."
"My dear fellow, who will let you?"
"That's not the point. The point is, who will stop me?"

— Ayn Rand, *The Fountainhead*

"Look If you had one shot, or one opportunity To seize everything you ever wanted, one moment Would you capture it or just let it slip?"

—Eminem, "Lose Yourself"

rest

A few months ago, I hurt my back.

It was, I'm sure, due to a slick pickleball shot where I served an ace and won the game (or maybe, probably, most likely, I just slept on it funny and woke up disheveled and broken).

Like any healthy adult, I whined about it a lot and shed some juicy crocodile tears to get my kids to make me dinner and bring me Coke Zero. (My oldest said it was too many trips up and down the stairs so HARD PASS. A dismal failure by all accounts.)

Injuries, as you well know, are only slightly more frustrating than having to wait a WHOLE WEEK for a new Ted Lasso episode. What's absolutely maddening is how deeply a setback like this can affect our daily lives–from the shoes we wear to how much weight we can lift, from taking clothes out of the dryer to how long we can stand on one leg to impress a gaggle of sixth graders. It even affects the energy it takes to unload the dishwasher (which is true, but I also just hate unloading the dishwasher).

BANANAS, I tell you.

Well, no mind. Since I am a chronic problem solver, I did all the things for my back: nursed it, rolled it out, got a massage, took some heavy narcs (jk, Mom), did a little voodoo magic, scaled back my exercise, and got excessively upset because no matter what I tried, it. wasn't. getting. better.

Seems like a cruel joke. This literal back pain was turning out to be a pain in my figurative backside. I couldn't move or lift or stand or sit or do damn well anything besides impress others with my wit and charm.

Now, I'm not ordinarily a "don't mind me, I'm going to spiral into an oblivion of helplessness" kind of gal (yes, I am). But damn it all to hell, after weeks of responsible adult behavior of taking care of my problems, I soon felt an inordinate amount of pressure and misappropriated guilt at the length of time my loser body was taking to heal. A TERRIBLE BLEEPING WASTE OF MY LIFE! Specifically, I felt as if I was losing precious moments of productivity and years of progress. I was just losing, would lose, had lost everything I'd worked so hard to earn.

OH KIERA, YOU GOT ME AGAIN. THIS ISN'T REALLY ABOUT INJURIES, THIS WAS A PLOT TO GET ME TO READ MORE.

Oh, people of the world, I wish you could see the inside of my mind. Splatters of neon like the backlights of a classic skating rink, the brightness of ambition shining like the stage on Broadway. Breakthroughs and intuition, what-ifs, outgrown truths, and so. much. growth. plaster propaganda along the gentrified walls of my brain.

I am fueled by two fires: progress and productivity.

And somewhere along the winding, slippery trail of confusion that was my youth, I found myself believing what I thought was the absolute truth: productivity and progress are synonymous. That they are two sides of the same coin, irrefutably connected together in a sort of eternal chicken-and-egg conundrum.

To make progress, I must be productive.
While being productive, I must make progress.

Rinse. Repeat.

These fires burn inside me, plead with me, beg me to fulfill as much of my potential before it's too late. *Your future is so bright*, they whisper, *but you're running out of time.*

And, oh, baby. Cliché cultural norms back me up. *You get what you work for, not what you wish for*, whispers the sense of urgency that now dictates my thoughts. *Do or do not, there is no try. Go big or go home.*

And so, I fill my time. I double-stuff my hours with work and duty and I exhaust myself in the hopes that one day, I will solve the equation of progress + productivity. *If I just work hard enough*, I believe. I glorify the busy because it will give me the progress I desire, and now I've become a machine: a machine of pluck and tenacity and persistence and determination.

I will burn both ends until I reach my potential.

And here's my admittance, a confession of absolute necessity:

I was wrong.

I'd forgotten to rest.

And I don't mean the kind of rest that lets us sleep deeply in between cool blankets late into a Sunday morning (although that's #1 in my book). I mean the kind of rest where mindfulness exists. The rest that gives you permission to turn your brain off and sit without needing to be productive in the moment. No personal bests, no reaching for the stars, no platitudes.

A creative rest. A physical rest. Mental, emotional, and spiritual.

I resist rest.

Rest, I've assumed, denotes laziness and complacency. See, I grew up with the fear of laziness deep in my bones; it permeated my body like the humid cold of Indiana winters. The idea of laziness has always plagued me like a sickness, an illness of ignorance.

Maybe, in fact, I don't know how or from what to rest. Maybe I don't know what it is or what it looks like. Maybe it camouflages itself as something else, and I'd never recognize it if I saw it.

I hope I find it.

Rest gives us time to recover.
To heal.
To grow.
To sit.
To see.

Rest rejuvenates us to start again, breathing
clarity into a cluttered mind.

A true rest is a reset, helping renovate
its place inside your mind.

I want the rest that helps give me the grace to simply
be okay.

Rest is no waste of time.

Rest is, simply,
time.

compliments

"Um, hi. You are SO BEAUTIFUL," I said, my jaw dropping into my chicken enchilada.

Our waitress blushed as she handed us two glasses of Diet Coke, limes wedged onto the rims.

"Thank you?" she mumbled, sheepishly.

"She's not hitting on you," clarified my friend, Morgan. "She literally does this all the time."

Guilty.

My big mouth is not exclusive to beauties serving up chips and salsa. Compliments could roll for the gal in the carpool line with a sweet mohawk, cashiers at seedy gas stations, construction workers with giant biceps, students with excellent comma usage, the guy with cool kicks on the frontage path along the Grand Canyon, the squad getting high scores at Top Golf, et al. Also at risk for being awarded my accolades are those at art shows, airports, Trader Joe's, batting cages, etc.

Once, I saw the most handsome guy I'd ever seen.

"In case no one told you today," I began, helicopter blades churning furiously in my abdomen. "You're very handsome."

Then I ran away very, VERY quickly.

Compliments don't have to be romance-novel steamy or written as a power ballad or accompanied with sleazy winks — just a little nudge that says, "Yo. Here's looking at you today."

Our society is very, very good at hiding. We hide behind computer and phone screens, behind the glorification of "busy" as we fit in jobs, exercise, kids, and a decent soda addiction. This awkward confidence for being able to talk to anyone can be, admittedly, uncomfortable where attention is perhaps unsolicited. We hide in our toasty corners of comfort, and it's a lot easier to get by without looking.

Without seeing.

There's no blame. No shame. Just a lot of cool opportunities that have the potential to be missed.

So, here's a challenge. Tell *one* person today something cool about them. Send a text, a DM, or a ransom-type letter (don't really ask for a ransom, though). Compliment the smell of someone's gym bag or give a thumbs up to the grocery store clerk for her neato glass eye.

Put your phone down. Look up.

Who do you see?

the ones who let go

Rubber soles of our sneakers echo on the gym floor
as chalked hands pull on the coarse rope
between abraded palms.
We pit strength against strength in an elementary game
designed for war–
to preserve power,
to struggle for supremacy.
A conquest for control.

We protect our own,
the ones on our side
of the demarcated divide.
The rope, impossible to hold onto,
rips through our raw hands

but we hold on.

Should we slip or should we fall,
we will lose it all.

———————————

Do war champions win by strength alone?
Or do they succeed by the sticky stratagem devised to
outfox a fox
as we play not to out-muscle our enemies,
no,
but to wear them down
in burden and exhaustion
until the rope slips through inflamed, bleeding palms.

Until they fall,
humiliated and
defeated.

We celebrate the victors
when we should consider instead their challenger,
one who held on for the fates of many,
one stronger than they
because
she
or he
or me
knew it was time to let go,
worn down by the constancy of change,
holding the weight of enduring,
holding the weight of protecting her own—
the Atlas of her own world.

And if the victors had eyes to see,
and I mean really see,
they'd run to bandage her bleeding hands,
patch her skinned knees,
reach down and help carry her weight,
her burdens,
her impossibilities,
and hold her sorrows in the crooks of their arms
as she rests.

She could lay shattered there,
a fallen relic,
but instead –
instead of tears
instead of disrepair
instead of never being enough,
compassion breathes life into her battered soul.

The one who lets go —
she is you
and she is me.
The wars that could break us
instead bond us,
and she can stand up
again
again
again.

a recurring dream:

A celebration.
For me.
Awarded for my auspiciousness.
Stage lights and eloquent introductions.
Expensive, tailored pants and book signings.

I'm late.

Lead fills each vein and capillary.
Strength drains from me with each step.

I speak.

My words are broken.

I sign.

My pens are dry.

I see the crowd checking watches,
shaking heads.
Inconvenienced by their wasted time.

"I'm right here!" I scream.
But fear whisks away my voice.

The stage lights go dark.
The seats are empty.
And I am forgotten.

remember tonight.

Remember the guilt that wraps my heart with sinewy ropes, slowing its beats but quickening panic in bursts of ragged breathing. The rush of self-reproach breaks the dam of calm inside my chest, and I wonder if I'll ever get used to the discomfort.

Remember the anxious footsteps echoing down the hall. She clambers onto my lap, her limber legs kicking my shins as she appropriates my space as hers. "Mom, come play with me," she begs. Her eyes, hoping for trampolines and popsicles and Lego towers, dull as I murmur generic wait-a-minutes and hold-on-a-seconds, promises that are rarely kept.

Remember then the silence. Tepid, unresponsive. The flatness in the air as my girls, stocked away in their beds for the night, grow alone in the rooms next to me.

Remember this feeling that I. am. not. enough for the world to read or hear or know the words that light up my mind like brilliant show marquees, the currents of metaphors running electricity through my system.

Remember the desperate need for raw validation from trusted, intimate friends who told me, "Kiera. Write. You have to write."

Remember this moment. The presence of this time demands an impossible recompense — a cost for which I've cried, fought, craved, and paid. Never offhandedly or casually.

Remember this, as I sit on my unmade bed, my mind occupied with unfolded laundry and broken sprinkler heads. I've not yet learned how to ignore the insistence of that which matters the least.

Remember tonight.

These are the reasons I write.

trampoline parks

I'm a writer, I told her.

She was a stranger with red hair and a friendly smile, a mom like me, keeping tabs on children bouncing their way through a crowded trampoline park. We connected quickly over laughter and exorbitant ounces of fountain Diet Coke, which we slurped through straws.

For fifteen minutes, she and I conversed about the ho-hum–the redundant and rehearsed first date minutiae about kids and homes and families, and whom we would French if we were absolutely forced to kiss a celebrity.

"What do you do for work?" she asked.

A teacher. Sixth grade. My fifth year teaching. Yes, it's hard. Yes, we need subs. No, I don't get paid a lot.

I paused, feeling the familiar broil of insincerity bubble inside me. I'd been sitting on it, hiding it away, burying myself beneath monotony or mayhem so I don't have to face the fear of rejection, the burden of failure, the gut punches of keyboard warriors who dissect and break apart those who try to penetrate the world with a word or two.

Ten years ago, I ran a marathon. "I'm not a runner," I insisted to everyone who expressed pride or congratulations until my neighbor looked me in the eyes and said, "Why do you keep saying that? You run. You are a runner."

I breathed in deeply, inhaling and exhaling the truth that seemed too scary to be the truth — the truth that fueled my days and my nights, the fire that I could feel burn me from the inside out.

I am, in every way, my truth.

"I'm a writer," I told her.

Vulnerabilities leaked from punctures in my battered soul. No longer a stranger, she caught in her hands the very reasons why I've been hiding from my potential. Why I protect myself and cradle my emotions in the confines of an iron cage around my scarred heart. Why all the while my heart is a heavy beat drop as I seek to fling my words off the highest skyscraper like an explosion of confetti.

Why is she the person I told? Why is her voice the one to which I listened?

A stranger with red hair and a friendly smile.

"Publish your book," she said.

I step back to see, part I

Haphazardly splattered words drip down
the blank canvas, pooling in puddles
of pronouns and prepositions.

Using freehand strokes, I brush subtly into
story arcs and drench diction with color and
blend. Nuances move and dance across the
canvas, generating the silhouette of a story.

The narrative evolves as clean neutrals tincture sable
darks, balancing the whole and blending whimsy with
grief, peace with predicament, conflict with resolution.

I see where the calm, smooth
brushstrokes create lyrical fluidity.

I see the smears of abstract anger, the
jarring frenzy of dissonance, the vehemence
that drips without direction.

I see a story.

Brewing along the shadowy edges of the canvas,
however, the dark remains untouched.

Perhaps it's sacrilege to tidy with faux sanguine
those corners of the dark, where hurt and
ache sit resolutely in pain and power.

Perhaps it's the density of the paint, laden with
burden, that demands a quiet respect.

Perhaps the dark gives power to the light.

Drafts rewritten and revised and ignored,
layers beneath a finality that blends
and flows into rich congruence.

I rework semantics, using a proverbial putty
knife to apply a thick, gritty texture so I can
cover the mistakes and the words that burn.
The words that I can't quite let others see. The
words that perhaps conceal the real art.

One day, I'll use less texture.

I sit and stare at the work that has consumed me.

Like the petals on a daisy – I hate
it. I love it. I hate it. I love it.

I feel brave.

I shut the MacBook.

i step back to see, part II

I wither in anxiety.

Fear cripples my thoughts, paralyzing me.

Did I write too much?
Are my words too much?
Will someone read this?
Will I matter?

Ensnared by the Ferris wheel of vulnerability, I panic as I fly higher. Higher. I grip the edge of my seat as the frenzy inside me whispers to break down the art I have carefully constructed.

Delete the post.
Erase the story.
Hide.

"Kiera," I whisper. "Do not open the Macbook."

Busy myself.
Busy myself.
Busy myself.

I feel the quiet seep in. Self-compassion dissipates the panic and fear.

I've come full circle.

I get off the Ferris wheel.

With nothing but the tools of an artist, I begin
again, a blank canvas before me, begging
for nuances and texture and depth.

The words come.

And I splatter paint.

nothings

Write something.

Write something.

Write something.

Nothing.

Nothing.

No thing.

Some thing.

What if my words aren't things, but are

brush strokes against canvas,
raindrops collecting in ditches.
intricate notes in a melody.

What if even my nothings are something?

for: mom

Don't feel down!
Life is hard.
You can never expect what's going to happen to you.
Sometimes you can find yourself trying to give up.
Don't.
Keep moving forward, even when things get frustrating.
Don't stop.
You can do whatever you want to if you just believe.
Believe in yourself.
You can do it.
Follow the path leading to success.
If you make a mistake, don't think about it. Move on from it.
Mistakes are GREAT.

Love,
Your daughter

the freedom of failure

One of the most underrated animated films is the 2007 Disney movie, *Meet the Robinsons*, which is totally heartwarming and a super important reminder that adults and children alike should echo the movie's theme to "keep moving forward."

In a particularly poignant scene, Lewis, a brilliant child inventor, hangs his head in shame and apologizes profusely when his dual peanut butter-and-jam configuration, well, jams, and explodes chunky JIF all over his quirky but welcoming hosts.

Immediately, he is greeted with enthusiastic applause.

"YAY!" they all shout, "YOU FAILED! It was AWESOME! EXCEPTIONAL! OUTSTANDING!"

Failure is absolutely brilliant.

Stick with me. I know it doesn't always FEEL brilliant.

Circa 1200 AD, in addition to the first buttons, eyeglasses, and the mind-blowing Fibonacci sequence, the word "failure" erupted into existence, coined to explain being unsuccessful in accomplishing a purpose.

Wait. That's it? Unsuccessful in accomplishing a purpose? On that note, I fail every day to wake up on time, not buy useless items at Costco, or limit my cookie intake.

Yes, of course, we could hem and haw over its many definitions and uses and word progressions and blah, blah, blah. My point: Over the last 800 measly years, we (society) have really done a number in damning ourselves with a tainted version of what failure means. It's as if we've decided to apply an oily, viscous version of failure to our intrinsic worth, an ointment that harms more than it helps, and it sits, untouchable, sticky, staining, and demanding.

And now, many fear failure, its processes, and the weight of its social implications.

We blacklist our ideas, dreams, and "un-successes" as unworthy or stupid, we pour out our hearts and minds simply for the nod of someone's approval, and we demand an impossible perfection from others and ourselves.

We wear failure's swollen, seared brand upon our breasts like a scarlet letter; for what purpose? As a condemnation for simply trying something that might not work? How dare people try out their unnatural, odd, and BRILLIANT, POTENTIALLY LIVE-SAVING ideas because, ew, what if they fail?

How embarrassing.

It seems like humans really miss the mark sometimes.

Instead, try something with me.

Let's rebrand failure.

Let's rewire our cognitive circuitry and let failure *in* instead of pushing it *out*. Let's embrace the idea of making mistakes, starting over, changing our minds, adding and taking away, burning, building, breaking, and bridging.

You have what is left of THIS life–let's not waste the rest of it with maudlin responses or feel-good bromides to failed attempts.

Let's demand that failure sit hand-in-hand with self-compassion, resilience, and the pursuit of imperfection. Failure is beautiful and brave —you deserve every chance to try and try and try again. Here's to moving forward.

So, a round of applause for you, and you, and you. You did it!

You failed.

breakable

Humpty Dumpty once sat on a wall.

That's how the story begins, anyway. We sing, we clap, we teach phonemic rhyming patterns to preschoolers about tragedy befalling breakfast food. (beFALLING?? I'm brilliant.)

Now, I'm by no means a literalist. But our friend H. Dumpty? First of all–not an egg. Although coined as such by author Lewis Carroll in his classic, *Through the Looking Glass,* I really think ole' Louie was just, like, hangry for an omelet or something. Instead, Humpty D. was most likely – alleges fact-friendly and verifiable Wikipedia – a massive iron cannon used in England in the 1600s.

Can you imagine the back-breaking effort, the simple machinery, and the number of stocky, caffeine-laden CrossFitters required to set this Herculean brute atop a wall as a protection, a guard, an artillery powerhouse against enemies?

However, as history or herstory (depends on the version?) attributes, a surprise blast — an explosion of crippling force — knocked this impenetrable guard down and out of commission.

Thus, the Humpty Dumpty who once sat on a wall had a great fall.

A great fall, the rhyme says. The kind that we remember by distinct smells and specific words and exact moments in blinding lights and frustratingly slow motion. A fall that knocks the wind out of our chests, suffocating us momentarily as we gasp for breath and struggle to orient ourselves with stings of pain and already-forming bruises.

A fall that breaks us.

I imagine her feeling her own immeasurable weight, suspended in the air as her foundation was blown from underneath her.

Yes. Although linguistically masculine in gender, I attribute heaviness and powerful force to the "she" pronoun. She, who inexplicably feels the weight of her own fragility and holds tight to the empathy for others. She, with exponential feelings of an uncomfortably large size, who felt her wall of validity and identity fall out from under her. She, who, due to gravity and force, came tumbling down without the inertia or support to reverse. Why was her wall crumbling? What happened? What could she have done differently? Why wasn't she enough?

She, who feels the complicated burdens of inadequacy without realizing that she fell, because sometimes WE FALL.

And so there she lay, in piles of her own emotional debris. Broken. Bruised.

But not alone.

Assessed. Documented. Analyzed. Fiddled with. Pieces of her jammed back painfully into tender, swollen sockets. Misshapen. The fixers tinkered with their tool belts, but alas, they couldn't put her back together again. Hazardous. A loss. Unfixable. Written off. After they shook their heads and click-clicked their tongues in elitist pity with hushed murmurs of "that's too bad," and "such a shame," they left her, broken and rusty on the grass.

And the nursery rhyme ends.

How wildly disappointing.

But

this isn't the end of her story.
Of your story.
Of my story.

Silently, without attention or fanfare, people found her in the rubble. Her people, her village, came to her. They sat with her. They wept with her. They gave genuine compassion and empathy and love, and cared tenderly for her cracks and breaks. They held her gently and soothed her and kissed her forehead as she called out in pained cries; they removed shrapnel and pieced together fragments of her weary soul that were shattered in the blast, that broke as she fell. Pieces of her that would never look or feel the same again.

I want to whisper a secret to you.
To my girls. To myself.

It's okay to break.

We were absolutely designed to be breakable.

The gravity of our and others' missteps, our precariously-balanced emotional equilibriums, our internal calibrations that hover in survival mode — we WILL inevitably fall. And with every step we take each day, either timid or bold, we know with experiential knowledge that everything we believe to be true — the walls we sit upon, our fortresses, our foundations, our bastions — could change.

Everything. And it's okay.

It's okay to sit on the highest wall.
It's okay to have a great fall.
It's okay to hurt and to break and to change.
It's okay to get back up.
It's okay to do it all over again.

As tragically complex as our bodies, our minds, and our hearts may be — oh, how deliciously resilient and hardy they CAN be.

Eventually, quietly, relentlessly, painfully, we will feel the peaceful signs of healing. The moments of growth that show us just how far we have come. Just how much fear we've faced. Just how much we wanted to overcome. We see the scars fading and we feel a semblance of wholeness. A different wholeness altogether–one that encompasses new experiences and grief and turmoil, but also readily available empathy and compassion. And now is where we climb to even higher heights, breathing in the clear air from the snowiest peaks of the highest mountains.

We must be stronger and braver now.

And always still breakable.

Resilience

a crash course in resilience

The April morning in northern California's Henry W. Coe State Park proved clear and warm, projecting sunny skies late into the afternoon. Having rented a mid-grade mountain e-bike from a local sports store, I felt fluttery and inexperienced as I suited up, pulling on elbow and knee pads to protect my aging joints from significant injury in my first attempt at mountain biking.

My zealous biking partners, all of whom had ridden these trails before, ranged in patience levels that morning as they gave me a crash course in mountain biking before we began our moderately difficult fourteen-mile excursion to nowhere. We kicked off, splashing through rocky creeks and winding steep switchbacks as we ascended 2,300 feet over the next seven miles.

Fast forward: I spent the next six hours completing my own crash course in mountain biking.

I stumbled up thin, single-wide trails, rammed into steep side cliffs, spun out on gravel, applied too much brake and not enough brake trail after trail, flipped off my bike, barely missing being impaled by errant tree limbs, fell down the side of a small, grassy mountain, and, as any newbie biker knows, my backside bruised quite nicely. Sitting was a struggle.

I fell. Again and again and again.

I listened to my co-bikers advise me on new strategies and adjusted speeds. I slowed down, walked down difficult passages, changed body positions, tried to trust my bike and, more importantly, trust its rider.

Don't worry — I kept falling.

In one spectacular display of amateurism, I flipped off the side of my bike and landed on top of ripped-down tree limbs on the side of the trail, breaking them violently into scraps of kindling under my body weight. The shock of falling sang panic through my system, and I lay on the dusty gravel and cried.

"Are you okay?" shouted a gruff voice behind me.

I nodded, wiping hot tears off my face.

"You're going to be okay," he said firmly.
"Just keep getting back up."

I pulled my aching body back onto my bike and kept going, the sun warm on my back.

It's a commonplace story, really. The classic tale of resilience: falling and getting back up. Being able to bounce back. It's a plucky little measure of feel-good advice we use to encourage those around us. We preach resilience to our children, to our schools, to our friends and families: You can do hard things. Never give up. Try again.

What about when we — you and me — fall?

Do we abide by the same precepts
we use to teach others?

Nah–I don't. I pack rocks of self-criticism in
my own backpack to weigh me down in self-
sabotage as I sink in an aimless sea.

What? It's true. I'm working on it.

I trap myself in my own mind with worries
and anxieties completely out of my control
and lockbox myself in without a shred of self-
generosity. I tie myself to the proverbial railroad
with an incoming choo-choo in the distance as I
scream at myself to "GET OFF THE TRACKS!"

I told you. This is not an advice book.

At times, we become haters worse than the trolls
of the internet, bullies with brilliant self-inflicting
hooks and uppercuts. We become victims to the
enemies inside our own minds, the voices of self-
loathing that confuse and berate, taunt and provoke.

Quit that shit.

Thus far, you've had a 100% success rate of
overcoming challenges. You're sitting here
reading this, aren't you? No refunds.

Bet on yourself, not the enemies in your mind.

I hope you fall. I hope you fail. I hope you sink in
an aimless sea and have to figure out how to let
go of the rocks you shoved in your backpack.

I HOPE YOU KEEP GETTING BACK UP.

part 7:
finding the fighter

"You're broken down and tired
Of living life on a merry go round
And you can't find the fighter
But I see it in you so we gonna walk it out
And move mountains
We gonna walk it out
And move mountains...
And I'll rise up
High like the waves
I'll rise up
In spite of the ache
I'll rise up
And I'll do it a thousand times again."

— Andra Day + Jennifer Decilveo, "Rise Up"

naked

One soulless November day, confusion and worry exploded from my anxious mind, their fragments striking my repetitive existence like shrapnel.

I wrote down one complicated thought after another, a series of provocative doubts that threatened the survival of my current, perhaps inauthentic, self.

For months, I had been opening my eyes to new ideas and freedoms that could help me break free from the confines in my life, the ones I had clung to for the sake of tradition and duty. Breaking away from my comfortable past would catapult me into a world of the delicious and terrifyingly unknown, landing me on an unfamiliar trail of self-discovery. I was heading toward a wild expanse of instinctual architecture, brick after brick built for me and by me, with a permanent mortar cementing my changes–

there would be no going back.

I was scared.

I didn't know if I was ready to abandon decades of familiarity, to seek uncharted challenges in pursuit of potential, or to trust my own instinct as my guide. I felt naked and exposed, shedding the skin that no longer fit the now stronger, more definable me.

I whispered these fears to a friend who held no judgment, no condemnation, no selfish motive, but who instead held space for the cautiousness and yearning I felt.

His response:

"I think you actually know the answer.

Don't settle. You are way too everything to settle."

change

We drove eastbound along I-40 too early in the morning, before the truckers had even finished their morning coffees. A long, absolutely boring stretch of Arizona lay ahead of us that day, the highway pocketed only by overpriced gas stations and side-of-the-road turquoise jewelry stands. I made small talk (I am consistently chatty) and mentioned offhandedly that, "wasn't it crazy that a giant canyon in the ground was only a mere 58 miles north of this decrepit desert?"

"I've never been to the Grand Canyon," he said.

So we went to the Grand Canyon.

It was an impromptu change that added about 4 ½ hours onto our drive that day, one that allowed us to collect about a million and a half memories.

And I absolutely loved it. I CRAVE the adventure of change.

The excitement, the challenge, the newness. I want the dips and turns, the thrills of rocketing too far into the sky and the fear from the stomach-flopping drops that make us second-guess ever straying this far outside of our comfort zones.

It's the problem-solving that I love. The questioning. The asking and searching and tinkering and

fixing. Feeling the validity of every emotion.
Fear. Anxiety. Pride. Growth. Fear again.

Change is so meticulously unreliable. It requires
courage and a keen eye to notice the bypaths we
could-should-would take to learn and grow and
become a more seasoned version of ourselves.

Change demands failure. So much failure.
In return, however, we have to practice
grace and self-compassion, which I believe
we fear more than the failure itself.

We overdo it. We underdo it.

Days of productivity. Believing so deeply in ourselves
that we could burst. Palpable resilience and power.
But then nights of anxiety. All the brain blocks. Letting
those little voices in that whisper, "Yeah, right. You?"

Deciding you are brave enough to swim the
currents of change is crucial. Being willing to
fail and learn and fail and learn and fail again is
the only way to be able to look back and say,

"Damn. I am stronger. I am braver. I am the
best version of myself that I've ever been."

Take the drive. Make the change.

Put this book down.

Go take one tiny step in the direction of the best version
of you. Pick me back up and write what you did. Tell me
all about it.

like iron

Today, my friend asked me if the pain of heartbreak and grief ever gets easier. Can we really overcome the pain of the past?

A valid question, my dear, for all of us.

To "overcome" means to prevail.
To win. A triumph in full.

Perhaps I once believed that overcoming grief meant ridding myself of the ache that sat so unbudging and permanent inside my chest. The only way to heal, I thought, was to relegate that ache as a dusty relic of the past, or to beat it, like a character in a video game.

I was wrong. That's okay.

I have no interest in defeating grief.

Instead, I want to exist within it, to give the refining fire of grief ample room in my heart.

Not because I'm afraid of it.

Like fire, grief has a consumable power to destroy, to cause destruction and devastation in its wake.

However, fire also fortifies. Intense, powerful fire can temper structural metals, such as iron and steel, decreasing their hardness, yes, but making them even stronger and more flexible under intense pressure.

This strengthening process gives us the ability to absorb emotional aftershocks and crucial pain points with our fortification through the power of grief.

Grief can take, but grief can also give.

Let it do its work.

"I don't think it gets easier," I replied to my friend. "But we get stronger."

In this way, we win.

A triumph in full.

the rise and fall of loneliness

I crave it.

Until I don't.

Time without distractions. Time to think, to prepare, to ponder, to process the thoughts that sit in the wings, impatiently waiting for their turn to take center stage.

I am content with who I am. Content with the progress and the mistakes and the beauty of my reality, and I'd like to imagine that I feel no urgency for busyness or engaging in repetitive social interaction in order to fill voids inside my heart and soul.

But human connection pulls me in, reaching for my hands. It grabs me by my lapels, even around belt loops as I feel pulled to find someone who can hold all of my weight in their unyielding arms.

Come with us, the whispers of attachment echo in the empty chamber of a lonely heart.

And I find that, yes, I connect with others to feel intimacy, to feel whole, to say everything and absolutely nothing at all.

And when I feel full, I step back again into the shadows of time alone.

I write. Until I hear the whisper again and feel the weight of loneliness burden my soul.

sea glass

The remnants of a glass bottle,
discarded on rocky shores.

Sharp, rigid slivers of glass threaten the uncalloused
heels of unsuspecting passersby, those searching
for creatures that lurk in tide pools. Abandoned
in plain sight, each carelessly broken shard
could leave others hurting and scarred.

Unyielding and dangerous.

Repetitive waves of salty seawater hit
powerfully against the rocky shores
where the broken bottle remains.

Pulls me out with the tide. Drags me in the sandy
undercurrent and pushes me back again.

Back. Forth. Buries me deep in the rush of the
undertow. Pushes me against the rock.

I'm drowning. Exhausted at being
beaten back and forth.

Time moves slowly.

I settle into the monotony of the to and fro,
the pummel, and the moments of relief
before feeling the bashing of thousands of
pounds of water weighing down on me.

I am tossed back to the rocky shore,
where I dry in the warm sun.

I hurt less. I feel less piercing pain at my
shattering. I settle in the space around me.

My edges have been whittled down by
time, by sand, by wind, by water;

I am not so sharp and broken anymore.

Instead, I am translucent and beautiful,
broken but smoothed by pain and grief.

I am a treasure, sought after by
heels of uncalloused feet.

I am sea glass.

queen of hearts

What if the Queen of Hearts sits on a
throne of fear instead of rage?

Maybe her inadequacies and what-to-dos shuffle
into decks of numbered worries that become
the fierce protectors of her vulnerability as
she wanders throughout her wonderland.

Maybe she weeps freely at the demands of caring for
a nation, her tears carving out deep, cavernous space
with each lament, preparing the way for another ocean
of tears by a girl not entirely unlike the queen herself.

Maybe she never healed from a triggering heartache
that blinds her periphery and restrains her response
of sense and sensibility, so she rages and wages war
just to rid herself of the violent red inside her head.

Maybe she stares in the mirror at a woman so pierced
by proverbial thorns of worthlessness, unable to
bestow upon herself the same beauty and purity
as the white roses she grows in her garden.

Maybe she only knows how to stay wounded, fearful,
and fearsome, knows no other way to lead than to
mislead, trailing residual uneasiness behind her.

What if she's not the villain after all?

mixed paint

Plums.
Shades of sunshine.
What is the color of falling in love?
Ocean blues and jade greens.
Charcoal in shadows
with a tinge of wildflowers.

I've been stuck in a palette of primary colors.

Trapped.
Inside the box
Inside the paint chip

Inside inside inside

Where are the hues?
the nuances?
the shadows?
the contrast?

Show me something more than I've been.

You've mixed me.
A new color.

No box.
No fine outlines.

Push me around a stretched canvas
 and see me mix with what was and what will be.
Watch me cover the old.
Cover me. Uncover me. Texture me.

New color.

Mix me.

a total loss

"I'm sorry, but your vehicle was deemed a total loss," the insurance agent said, his Carolina drawl ironically unapologetic.

A total loss.

The verbiage sat funnily on my tongue, like rotten fruit – tingly and sickeningly sweet.

A total, complete, irrevocable loss.

It must be this way, I suppose. The well-oiled machine of evaluation must take into consideration actuarial algorithms, collision repair reports, and market approximations so that a stranger can dictate the terms of damage that, tsk-tsk-tsk, just can't be recovered.

Emotionless box-checking.

Check.
Check.
Check.

A total loss.

Interesting words, don't you think?

A total loss where my girls and I logged 64,437 miles of cross-country adventures from California beaches to the forested edges of Vermont. We wound along the frontage of upstate New York, where America flirts with Canada, wandered through waves of endless grain, and counted cacti in the southwestern desert heat. We skated across salt flats, curved through canyons, and battled Colorado blizzards, wiper fluid frozen in a whirlwind of white.

We stopped at a million gas stations for M&Ms and Coke Zero, carpooled to trampoline parks and pools, blasted "Fight Song" through open windows, wept while Jim Dale narrated Dobby's tragic death, and laid on the hood, watching satellites maneuver themselves around the big, big world.

This total loss has moved my little family from home to home, holding our unknown future inside the cardboard boxes of an old life. It shuffled my girls back and forth from mom's to dad's and back again, and held summer in its back pocket, the trunk littered with beach towels and sunscreen.

It accompanied me on first dates, acting as the safehold I needed to breathe through the plaguing nervousness that never goes away.

Miles and miles and miles of tears and fears, firsts and lasts, secrets and solitude. Where sometimes we talked, and sometimes we stayed silent.

Maybe it's a little silly, mourning a piece of metal en route to a junkyard, where total losses rust and rest.

But it's quite a loss to lose a total loss.

neon lights

The room was small but not uncomfortable.

I sat on a gray twill couch, flanked gently by summer throw pillows. Plucky pick-me-ups from the clearance section at TJ Maxx generously decorated tall walls of faux shiplap.

"Kiera, what do you want your future to look like?" my therapist asked.

I stared blankly at the dark Berber carpet and paused — not because I lacked words to answer the question. No, no. Rare occurrence, that.

I can see it.

My now, my past, my future. A spherical whole of encompassing color and light and hope.

Imagine, if you will, an amusement park at night. Bright neon lights break through crisp darkness, spinning smears of color. A million tiny lights resurrect the clunky, lifeless Ferris wheel. Nostalgic scents of funnel cakes and hot turkey legs, salty popcorn, and hardy, fragrant roses climb trellises and light poles. Screams of fear and laughter and glee, the click-click-click of the lift hill on a roller coaster, the clanking gears of carnival games all funneled into indiscernible chaos. We spin faster. We climb higher. We drop into weightlessness. Butterflies and adrenaline compete: Who will win? The nerves that keep us grounded, or the rush that catapults us?

"So," she repeats, "your future?"

I want the brightest lights in the darkest dark.
I want indiscernible chaos and the silence of listening
to a million thoughts.
I want nostalgia and memories and the tiny nothings of
the everyday.
I want laughter, so much laughter, and headaches from
when I cry instead.
I want the fear of falling and fluttering nerves, and the
loss of gravity when I drop without notice.
I want the rush of being scared, and I want to do it
anyway.
(And I want funnel cakes.)

My future isn't so much an If. It's a
When, plaited intricately with generous
strands of the past and the now.

The brightness and bravery and brilliance is in choosing
the future that fits
the complexity of me.

the fire i set myself

I've never permitted myself to be angry.

I've never felt worthy enough to hold anger's power.

Society and religion preach the danger in anger: hot-headed, aggressive, fiery, impatient, hostile, violent. Anger, I believed, belonged to those who stand on demarcated sides, throwing fists and spitting divisiveness, bruising egos across a line of no amends. Anger equaled self-righteousness and reactivity. Insidious ignorance. Cripplingly low self-esteem masqueraded as brutality, hurling insults.

Somewhere in my subconscious, I decided that anger belongs on a shelf, next to the bills that I'm ignoring, next to that faith box I was instructed to keep out of reach for all the unanswerable questions that plagued my soul.

I consistently chose the more rational, passive route of forgiveness and gratitude, which makes me sound like a saint. I've allowed myself a healthy period to cope with my grief and allowed myself to continue believing the best in others.

Fuck — I'm not a saint.

I thought I could fast-track the grief cycle without reaching inwardly enough to feel the sacred, heavy anger that filled the salient corners of my bruised and broken heart.

A hot, gritty fire rages inside my chest,
searing me from the inside out.

I'm angry.

I am violently angry. I'm angry at selfishness. At
the senseless tragedies that break the hearts
of real human beings with feelings and lives.

I'm angry that I've never been angry.

I'm angry that I've spent too many years protecting
the feelings of others instead of healing for
myself. That for the first time in my 37 years on
this earth, I am feeling the painful, cleansing,
and lasting effects of anger for the first time.

I am angry at myself for always
being SO GODDAMN NICE.

He cheated on me and I comforted him.
He cheated on me again and I soothed his heart.
He cheated on me again and I tried to make it work.
He cheated on me again and my heart broke.
He cheated on me again and I wondered
what I was doing wrong.

I'm angry at trust.

I'm angry at love.
I'm angry at feeling human.
I'm angry at my belief in others.
I am angry at the lessons I've tried to learn,
at the neediness I feel,
at the connections I desire,

at the patience I've allowed,
at the grace I've tried to give,
at those who want me to fit in a box of their making,
at those who second-guess my intentions,
at those who think they can control me.

Primal, cleansing anger burns me, and I collapse
into smoldering remnants of what once was.

I've spent years vying for others. For
their safety and their peace.

And now I'm vying for my own safety and peace.

For MINE.

For me.

And I will rise from the ashes.

to you.

I see you.

I see each brick. Heavy, enduring bricks molded from tumult and tragedy that you use to build the walls around you. I see you hide. I watch you bury yourself inside of the walls that will protect you from the weapons that have wounded you. Have weakened you.

I see the fatigue that drapes a weighted blanket over your shoulders, that sits heavy without hope for reprieve. I see dark eyes and smiles that don't quite reach your eyes.

I know the anxiety imploding inside your chest. The hopelessness that threatens to claw its way out. Self-compassion loses out to the daunting and absolutely overwhelming threats that you are. not. enough.

I see the fear and the worries that haunt you. The hows and what-ifs conspire against our fledgling resiliency and consume our visions for the future. How will we exist? How will we heal and trust? How will we open our mouths and hearts and hopes again?

I watch you cling to the falsities that you are unwanted. That you are broken. That you are alone. That you deserve this.

I watch you forget that you are, by nature, implicitly worthy. That you are powerful and grandiose and majestic.

I watch you shrink smaller to fit behind the walls you built. Walls expected by those who hurt and demand and force and control. Walls intended to hold the diminutive and weak.

No. No, no, no.

Look me in the eyes.

Scoot over. Make room for me.

I am sitting with you. I–she–he–we, who have felt these excruciating pains before. We, who, in the past, have constructed our own walls wherein to hide, give up, and accept loss and failure. We, who have learned over the course of our own lives all about shrinking to become small. We, who have learned the power of empathy and compassion of a few.

We will sit with you, and we will break this intolerable wall down together, brick by disused brick.

Make room for us.

Because you are never, ever alone.

part 8:
evolve or repeat

"He's fine. That's it. Nothing wrong with that, most people are fine. But it's not about him. It's about why the fuck you think he deserves you. You deserve someone who makes you feel like you've been struck by fucking lightning. Don't you dare settle for fine."

– Roy Kent, *Ted Lasso*

a montage of a boy or two

they said

you're much too gray to be completely pretty
but a younger you might make me want you

and see? those lips, too thin from passing their plump
along to pouty tweens
just don't call to me like the siren song
of the women i search for on the internet

and of course, i'm not attracted to you–
i whispered that into your ear
as i caressed your hair
and laid my hand on the small of your back

and i wish you could hear yourself–
or hear at all–
how embarrassing it is
to be next to the deaf girl

and do you see that if you want me to want you,
you'd rid your body of the imperfections around your
bra line
and erase the residual abdomen scars from growing
life
that no one needs to see
but you'd look so hot with larger breasts.

why don't you just take care of yourself, after all?

and if it was just you and not your kids, too–
i'd marry you.

and one day i gathered the reels of these memories,
sewn and grafted together
over the years of
forgetting my worth

there's no happily ever after
because i'm not a fairy tale or a figure to refigure.
i took the power away
and without their control,
the words crumbled
at my touch.

in hindsight

to the one who bought me cereal and hoped I'd sleep with him on his couch:
the best part of this date was the Nutter Butter cereal

to the one who said he'd buy me a trip to England if I played my cards right:
I don't play cards

to the one who said his semen had only ever been in one woman:
probably avoid using the word "semen" on future dates

to the one who took me shooting and bought me $80 protective ear muffs even after his bank card declined in front of me and he had to call his dad for money reinforcements:
this was singularly the most uncomfortable position I've ever been in.

to the one who enjoyed being suspended in mid-air by meat hooks gored into his shoulders:
BYE

to the one who told me he didn't know a woman was having sex with him until she had finished:
bullshit, stupid.

to the one who bought me snacks and left them on my car after work:
I never mentioned where I worked.

to the one who bought me wool socks from the outlet mall before our date:
very practical, thank you

to the one who told me that if it weren't for my kids, he'd marry me:
who said I wanted to marry you?

to the one who bought me an entire Costco pizza, 36 roses, 24 Mountain Dews, and 12 Crumbl cookies for one date:
tone it down, buddy.

to the one who bought investments and bid me farewell with a salute:
I still don't get this one

to the one who bought me Lululemon so I wouldn't embarrass him in my sweats at Walmart:
...it's Walmart.

to the one who said he'd pay for a boob job:
my boobs are in good hands, thanks

to the one who grilled expensive meat and then apologized for liking me:
this one was the wurst

to the one who came into my home and imprinted vulgar and menacing behavior onto my memories: fuck off, you sociopath

to the one who bought me bar stools on amazon: thanks?

to the ones who demanded selfie after selfie to prove they weren't being catfished: no and also no

to the one who said he'd buy me half a plane ticket to come to visit him: i've spent my whole life being half of someone's ticket. i want to be the entire ticket.

i choose this.

You see,
I could opt for the next man
who smiles genially at me
or who sends supermarket flowers,
frantically searching in desperation
for someone with whom to share a life
that he controls.
Someone, just someone,
who won't cause a scene
or speak too loud
or speak my own words,
but I get to pick
where we eat for dinner tonight.

I could settle for someone,
a generic anyone,
for a milquetoast sort of happiness,
based on trivial niceties
or evenings spent on opposite ends of the couch,
the television interrupting
lackluster conversations
as I wait
and wait
and wait
and wait
for passion to erupt.

I could face crippling betrayal
and lies
and lies
and lies

and lose my self-respect
as I beg him and beg him to stay
for us
for the kids
for the future and the past
as he waffles between what is best for him
and also
what is best for him.

I could shapeshift
for him
or him
or him,
dilute myself with ambiguity
so maybe
just maybe
he'll want me.
If I can just lose enough weight from trash diets
or mold myself from silicone to hide disgusting
imperfections
or become a fantasy from the images that arouse him
while his eyes stay closed,
and it's not me he sees.

I could be anything anyone wants me to be
and be
unloved
disrespected
controlled
unhappy
unchallenged

But instead
I choose this life.

I choose me.

a first date

This one was different from the others.

I leaned my black Chucks up against the
raw concrete wall, veined with natural
breakage from the settling foundation.

He sat next to me, at noon to my nine,
around the high bistro table, sipping his cider
and eating a turkey burger with egg.

His eyes scanned the exposed ceiling, metal pipes
labyrinthine through duct work and lumber.

"If you were stuck up there," he nodded to
the ceiling, "how would you get down?"

Fascinating.

We shimmied down industrial drain pipes in
date-night jeans and rock-climbed craggy
outcroppings of rough-hewn cement. We
landed softly on striped awnings and leapt
onto barrels of house-made pickles.

It was a first date.

A first date that broke the formality of cliché, stock-
photo dinners. That challenged previous meals with

blank smiles and nameless faces, championed by impersonal, vague, unimpressive conversation.

He. He. He.

He aroused my brain, my body,
my wit. He set me on fire.

He woke me up from the ennui of the status quo

 and I've felt alive ever since.

weight

I let my weight go,
lie on his chest
without reserve,
without fear.

I stop trying
to hold myself up,
to appear smaller
in flattering angles
with muscles tensed

and instead,
completely

sink

into

him

and let him hold me,
bear my every ounce –
all of me.

I am weightless
in his arms,
at our most intimate
as I shed my insecurities.

He collects them,
berries in a basket,
and keeps them out of reach

so I can rest.

a letter to a lover.

Good morning, love.

Had an idea.

How about we pack our weekend suitcases and pack the car with paddleboards and foam pads, the best kind of snacks, and drive and drive and drive until we get to where we want to go?

Start a fire.

Throw open the back doors.
Curl up under blankets and hear laughs echo through the mountains or get lost in the sound of crashing waves.
Laugh and love until we fall asleep.

Exhausted.

We can run away.

Come with me?

the end that is not really the end

"I stand here on the summit of the mountain.
I lift my head and I spread my arms.
This, my body and spirit, this is the end of the quest.
I wished to know the meaning of all things.
I am the meaning."

— Ayn Rand, *Anthem*

"In the end, we'll all become stories." - Margaret Atwood

I've been thinking lately about stories.

Where they come from and just how far they reach. How, in the pursuit of acceptance, we can doctor and fix and filter and enhance. Narratives broken apart into generalities.

And I
absolutely
don't don't don't
want a carefully curated collection of tidy words.

I want to tell stories of shattered hearts and broken dreams. The ache of acceptance. Raw hurt and loss.

The pain when I wasn't enough.

The grief. And fear. The suffocation of darkness and the unknown.

The bravery. Oh, girl. The bravery.
The laughter.
The smiles that touch the corners of our eyes.

Searching. Finding. Giving self-compassion.
Feeling confidence in authenticity.

Opening hearts and loving so hard. Loving so hard it changes you. Changes others.

Finding God-given peace.
Allowing that peace in.

Owning our bare, painful, and
utterly vulnerable progress.

Processing the change.

Embracing the unexpected. Living the answers to
questions we didn't even know we had been asking.

Feeling free.

My story isn't finished.

I am not finished.

Unfinished is the best kind of story, I think.